The Cube

The Ultimate Guide
to the World's
Bestselling Puzzle

Secrets
Stories
Solutions

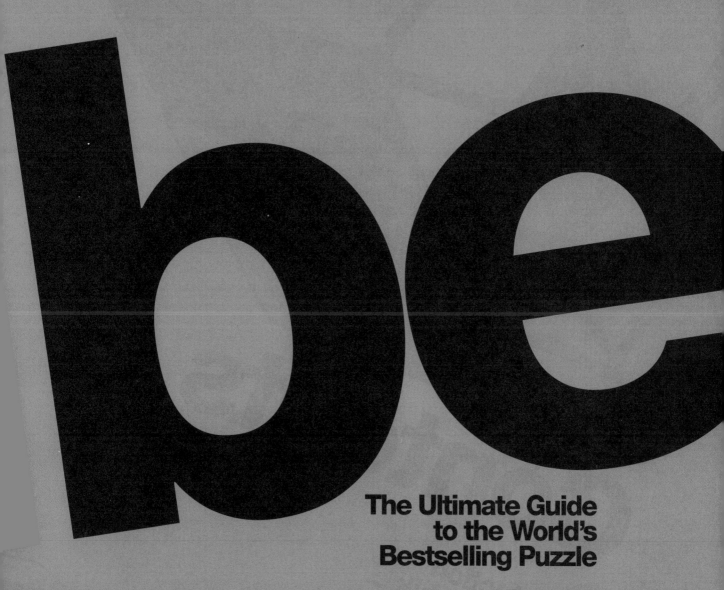

be

The Ultimate Guide to the World's Bestselling Puzzle

Secrets Stories Solutions

Jerry Slocum
David Singmaster
Wei-Hwa Huang
Dieter Gebhardt
Geert Hellings

BLACK DOG
& LEVENTHAL
PUBLISHERS
NEW YORK

Contents

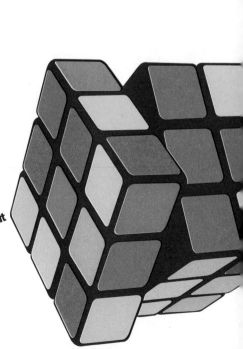

Black Dog & Leventhal Publishers
Hachette Book Group
1290 Avenue of the Americas
New York, NY 10104

www.blackdogandleventhal.com

Printed in the United States of America

Cover design & interior design by Andy Taray for Ohioboy Art & Design

RRD-C

First Edition: March 2009
10 9 8 7

Black Dog & Leventhal Publishers is an imprint of Hachette Books, a division of
Hachette Book Group. The Black Dog & Leventhal Publishers name and logo are
trademarks of Hachette Book Group, Inc.

The Hachette Speakers Bureau provides a wide range of authors for speaking events.
To find out more, go to www.HachetteSpeakersBureau.com or call (866) 376-6591.

The publisher is not responsible for websites (or their content) that are not owned by
the publisher.

Library of Congress Cataloging-in-Publication Data available upon request.

ISBN-13: 978-1-57912-805-0

Acknowledgments

We are very grateful to the many people who contributed so much to this book including the rotational puzzle designers that answered our many questions and contributed material on the puzzles they designed: Ernő Rubik, Larry Nichols, Uwe Meffert, Peter Sebestény, Panagiotis Verdes, Tony Fisher, Jean-Claude Constantin, Lee Tutt, Aleh Hladzilin, Katsuhiko Okamoto, Hidetoshi Takeji, Anthony Greenhill, Adam Cowan, Matt Shepit, and Drew Cormier.

Our special thanks to Ernő Rubik, Julie Shulick, Allan Slocum, Tim Slocum, and Lisa Tenaglia for editing the manuscript.

We sincerely thank our "Solving Team" of Julie Shulick, Allan Slocum, Tim Slocum, Annie Desjardins, Tyler Fox, Allison Frascatore, Tyler Hinman, Roger Manderscheid, David Mertl, Harold Raizer, Erik Sargent, Chris Shulick, Jack Slocum, and Lisa Tenaglia for trying and evaluating many versions of the Cube solutions and helping to improve their ease-of-use for beginners.

Dic Sonneveld contributed research on the history of the Cube.

Introduction

Back in 1974, not in my wildest dreams would I have imagined that in 2008 I would be writing an introduction to a book about the Rubik's Cube™. For me the 21st century was so far away and unforeseeable, it was like the setting of a science fiction novel. At the time, I knew the Cube was something very special and exciting, and that was enough for me. Discovering and understanding the idea is what kept me occupied—I was not interested in what would happen in the far future. I was busy finding the essence of my design—I worked just like the sculptor who chips the unnecessary layers off the stone in order to reveal its innate form creating the perfect design for the Cube.

Time has shown that two decisions I made over 30 years ago were the right ones. The first was to create an object in which content and form are in harmony—where space, form, dynamic structure, and appearance harmonize with human nature, body, and mind. The object had to have everything that is essential, no more, no less. My second decision was to share the result with the world. The achievement of this would prove to be the more difficult task. It took me a few months to design the Cube, but six years to find its worldwide distribution.

When I studied sculpture and architecture, I always felt some contradiction between Grand Art—art that manifests the thoughts and ideas of the artist with the techniques of fine arts and with no other function—and Applied Art—the connection to our everyday tasks in all fields of life and in which the factor of usability is important. This was probably the reason I finished my studies in a design school. I think the Cube is a result of my desire to create something that is between these two categories—or that represents both.

"Like other pieces of art, the Cube is more than itself. Though it may look very simple at first, it is in fact rather complicated and complex at the same time."

For me, the Cube is a piece of art. It is more than an object with the shape of a cube made of plastic, more than many colored stickers, more than a puzzle, and it is much more than a gimmick. Like other pieces of art, the Cube is more than itself. Though it may look very simple at first, it is in fact rather complicated and complex at the same time. Still in its beautiful complexity, despite its many transformations, it remains a single unit. What is really interesting for me, even today, is not my Cube as an object, but its relationship with the user and especially millions of cubes with millions of users (my estimation is over one billion people).

I admire Jerry Slocum's enthusiasm for puzzles and his ambition to popularize them. He has done an excellent job collecting most of the available materials in connection with the Cube.

Ernő Rubik, Budapest 2008

Chapter 1

Puzzle Crazes Before the Cube

By Jerry Slocum

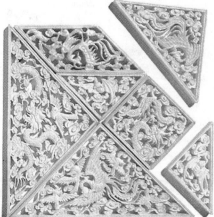

THE SEVEN PIECES OF THE IVORY TANGRAMS ABOVE AND TO THE RIGHT ARE USED TO FORM THE OVER 300 PROBLEM FIGURES IN *THE FASHIONABLE CHINESE PUZZLE* BOOK, BELOW.

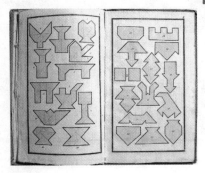

The Tangram 1817

Puzzle crazes are not new. People love to try their luck against elegantly simple mind-benders, and will spend a lot of time and money to do so.

The first international puzzle craze began in the early 19th century, when the Chinese invented the Tangram, a puzzle formed by dissecting a square into seven geometric pieces. A similar ancient rearrangement puzzle—a square piece of wood, cut into 14 geometric pieces—was discussed back in the third century in a letter written by the Greek philosopher Archimedes.

The pieces of the Tangram can be assembled to form thousands of different figures of people, animals, letters of the alphabet, and geometric shapes. The challenge is to assemble all seven pieces, without overlap, to form the figures.

The craze began after a pair of Chinese books were published in 1815, showing more than 300 problem figures and their solutions. Small boxed sets of the seven pieces made from carved ivory and wood were sent on trade ships to be sold in England, America, and Europe. The British published the first problem books outside of China early in 1817, and by the end of that year, *The Fashionable Chinese Puzzle* book had made the Tangram popular in London. It was copied throughout Europe and America, and soon new problem books were published throughout Europe.

Famous people and the masses were captivated by the puzzle. Napoleon Bonaparte, Lewis Carroll, Edgar Allan Poe, and Michael Faraday were fans of the Tangram. The German author C.L.A. Kunze commented, "This game, soon after its appearance, had become a favorite amusement in educated families of northern Germany. The examples came from England and were offered by Hamburg art dealers, and they were very elegant."

By early 1818, the French, Italians, and Germans created problems that were beautiful works of art, and Parisians in particular seemed to neglect everything else in life while solving Tangram problems. By 1840, the Tangram was being used as a fun way to teach children geometry and other subjects, and it continues to be widely used in schools throughout the world.

The 15 Puzzle 1880

The 15 Puzzle burst onto the market in Boston in 1880, and spread like wildfire to New York, San Francisco, and Europe. Still popular as a toy today, it consists of 15 numbered wooden blocks in a tray that would hold 16, leaving one empty space. The player dumps the 15 blocks out of the box, puts them back randomly, and slides them around, one at a time, to arrange them in numerical order with the vacant space after the number 15.

One reason that this simple puzzle became a huge craze is that, unbeknownst to many solvers, half of the random arrangements are mathematically impossible to solve. Try as they might, players found that about half the time, two of the blocks would end up in reverse order, such as the 15 and 14, and those two could not be reversed. After someone was successful at solving the puzzle, there was only a 50 percent chance that it could be solved on the next attempt. Newspapers and magazines throughout the U.S. wrote about the puzzle, rewards were offered to solve it, and many problems were caused by the intense fascination, including claims that the puzzle was driving people insane and more asylums were needed.

On February 23, 1880, *The New York Times* wrote in an editorial, "Certain obstinate people have been known to sit up all night at it, and still the numbers baffled them, for there is one certain combination which refuses 'to come right.' In a month from now, the whole population of North America will be at it, and when the 15 Puzzle crosses the seas, it is sure to become an English mania. In the meantime, it is the street vendors who are making a harvest out of the puzzle business." The editorial was amazingly accurate. The 15 Puzzle has continued to be quite popular ever since it was introduced, but modern versions in plastic and metal have the pieces constrained so they can not be dumped out and never are impossible to solve.

PUCK, AMERICA'S POLITICAL SATIRE MAGAZINE, USED THE 15 PUZZLE AS A METAPHOR FOR THE 1880 PRESIDENTIAL ELECTION.

NOYES P. CHAPMAN, INVENTOR OF THE 15 PUZZLE.

Credit for the puzzle's invention varied widely, from ancient civilization to a deaf student in Hartford, Connecticut, or a retired Civil War general in Iowa. *The Chester Daily Times* of Philadelphia commented, "The game of fifteen had more inventors than there are blocks in the box."

In January 1891, more than 10 years after the 15 Puzzle craze ended, America's greatest puzzle inventor, Sam Loyd, began a twenty-year campaign of interviews, articles, and puzzle columns claiming that he invented the 15 Puzzle. He took credit for not only the invention of the 15 Puzzle, but also Pigs in Clover, an 1889 dexterity puzzle, and the popular board game Parcheesi, which had been played in India as early as the fourth century. Even though he had nothing to do with the invention or popularity of the 15 Puzzle, Loyd's false claims convinced the world that he was the inventor until his hoax was exposed in *The 15 Puzzle* book, published in 2006.

The 15 Puzzle was actually invented by Noyes P. Chapman, a postmaster in Canastota, New York. One of Chapman's handmade 15 Puzzles was given to the American School for the Deaf in Hartford, Connecticut, and in June 1879, they began making the puzzles in the school's woodworking shop and selling them on the streets of Hartford and Boston. One of the puzzles made by the school was purchased in Boston in 1879 and given to Matthias Rice, who was looking for a product to be made in his woodworking shop. Rice began manufacturing the puzzle under the name the Gem Puzzle.

The puzzle started a craze and it continued until April 1880 in the U.S.. Even as Americans grew weary of the puzzle, the mania began in France and quickly spread through Europe. Almost a century later, Hungarian Ernő Rubik, while trying to improve the 15 Puzzle by designing a puzzle with no vacant space, invented the Rubik's Cube™ puzzle.

THE PIGS IN CLOVER PUZZLE STARTED A CRAZE IN 1889.

Pigs in Clover 1889

To solve the Pigs in Clover puzzle, the player uses dexterity to roll four clay marbles through a circular maze into a "pen" in the center. A huge craze resulted when the inventor, toy maker Charles Crandall, introduced it in February 1889. Three weeks later, *Waverly Free Press* reported, "The toy works are turning out 8,000 Pigs in Clover a day and are twenty days behind in their orders." The toy-history book *Toys in America,* by Ines and Marshall McClintock, described the spread of Pigs in Clover as "the best seller which swept over the country, and abroad to other countries, like a plague of locusts." Selchow and Righter, the distributor of the puzzle, was quoted as saying, "It is impossible to say how many will be sold before the craze runs its course, but a million puzzles probably falls short of the number."

Although Sam Loyd two years later claimed credit for inventing the puzzle, Crandall was granted a U.S. patent for Pigs in Clover in 1889, and all the contemporary newspaper articles and later books that describe the puzzle credit Crandall with the invention.

The first three mechanical-puzzle crazes took place in just over seventy years—1817, 1880, and 1889—but, it was another ninety years before the world would once again be caught up in a huge and amazing mechanical-puzzle craze. The rest of this book is devoted to the fourth puzzle craze: the story of the invention of Rubik's Cube™, its descendants, and the solutions for the family of rotational cube puzzles, 2×2×2 through 7×7×7.

JUDGE MAGAZINE USED THE PIGS IN CLOVER PUZZLE IN A POLITICAL CARTOON ABOUT THE DEMOCRATS TRYING TO RETURN TO THE WHITE HOUSE.

THE DEMOCRATIC "PIGS IN THE CLOVER" PUZZLE.

Chapter 2

The History of the Cube

By David Singmaster

THE 15 PUZZLE

EARLY INVENTIONS

When Ernő Rubik invented the Rubik's Cube™ in 1974, he knew he'd created an interesting puzzle, but had no idea that he was starting one of the greatest puzzle crazes of all time. His idea, however, of putting together a group of small cubes into a rotational puzzle was not necessarily original. A young man named Larry Nichols may have realized it first.

Growing up in the small town of Xenia, Ohio, Nichols loved games and puzzles, especially the simple mechanical puzzles he found in toy stores. One such toy was the 15 Puzzle. The puzzle had remained popular for over a century, and Nichols wondered if it could somehow be made more symmetrical and challenging without lessening its instant appeal.

In 1957, while strolling near his college campus one evening, he started thinking about ways to move small puzzle pieces without needing an empty space.

It suddenly occurred to him that there was no reason to limit the puzzle to flat squares. If little cubes were assembled into one large cube, there could be three axes of rotation passing through one beautiful and symmetrical puzzle—with no missing piece.

In 1959, while in graduate school at Harvard, Nichols made a few 2×2×2 puzzles, using small magnets to hold the cubes together so they could move. The models were a little hard to handle, but they immediately captured the attention of his friends and roommates. As he had hoped, eight pieces arranged in a cube were a lot more interesting and difficult than fifteen squares arranged in a tray. He discovered that twisting a corner cube 120 degrees produced arrangements that could not be solved, and he found sequences of moves that could be used to solve all the others and impress his friends.

Years later, while working for Molecu-Ion Research Corporation in Cambridge, Massachusetts, Nichols used the company's small machine shop to make an improved cube. Seeing it on his desk, Arthur Obermayer, the owner of the company, suggested that they apply for a patent and try to market the puzzle. They were granted a U.S. patent on April 11, 1972, about five years before Ernő Rubik's Hungarian patent. Nichols's patent is for a

2×2×2 cube with a magnetic mechanism, unlike Rubik's elegant mechanism that holds the pieces together.

From 1967 until 1972, Nichols and Moleculon tried to market the puzzle to leading U.S. game and puzzle manufacturers, including the Ideal Toy Corporation, with absolutely no success. In Ideal's opinion, the puzzle had three major problems: it was too hard to solve; two other cube puzzles, Soma and Instant Insanity, had saturated the market; and the magnets made it too expensive to produce and too easy to cheat.

Eventually the project was abandoned. However, in 1978, Nichols saw the Rubik's Cube™ marketed by Ideal Toy. Moleculon contacted Ideal and pointed out that they were infringing the Nichols patent. Ideal refused to acknowledge the patent and, in 1982, Moleculon filed a lawsuit against CBS, which had taken over Ideal, for $60 million in damages. In 1984, the case came to trial in the U.S. District Court in Wilmington, Delaware. After lengthy testimony, including four and a half days of testimony by Jerry Slocum, Moleculon's primary expert witness, the judge found in Moleculon's favor that Nichols' patent was valid and that Ideal had infringed on that patent. CBS appealed, and after many court battles, in April 1989, three judges sitting for the U.S. Court of Appeals found in favor of CBS.

Two other similar devices were issued patents before Rubik's invention. In 1960, a mathematics teacher named William O. Gustafson, in Fresno, California, invented the 2×2×2 Magic Sphere. Gustafson proposed a device with a central sphere with grooves, and in 1963, he was awarded a U.S. patent for his "Manipulatable Toy." Gustafson reportedly tried to market his sphere and was rejected by eighty companies.

Frank Fox of Buckinghamshire, England, filed for a U.K. patent on the "Amusement Device" on April 9, 1970. Fox's design consisted of a 3×3×3 puzzle in a sphere, using tongue-and-groove linking to hold the twenty-six exterior pieces together, leaving the center hollow. Fox intended to use this device as a kind tic-tac-toe board, though he mentions using twenty-six colors and letters and numbers.

LARRY NICHOLS

RUBIK'S EARLY 3×3×3
WOOD CUBE PUZZLE

ERNŐ RUBIK INVENTS HIS CUBE

Ernő Rubik was born in Budapest in 1944 to a prominent Hungarian family. His father, Ernő Rubik, Sr., was an aeronautical engineer who designed gliders and light aircraft and was awarded the Kossuth Prize in 1963, Hungary's highest honor. Rubik first studied sculpture but then shifted to architecture, earning a diploma from the Budapest Technical University in 1967. In 1971, he received a postgraduate diploma in interior architecture at the Academy of Applied Arts and Crafts, and became a lecturer at the academy.

In the spring of 1974, while he was teaching three-dimensional design, he had his epiphany. One of the standard exercises was to have students make cardboard cubes to show how cutting a cube in half each way produces eight cubes of half the size. The sides of the cube were colored so the relations between the large cube and the smaller cubes were clear. Rubik realized that turning one row of cubes would rearrange the smaller cubes, but re-form a large cube—and the concept for the puzzle was born.

The biggest challenge was designing a mechanism that would allow the rows of the cube to rotate. It was even more challenging than the puzzle itself. However, in about six weeks, Rubik devised the mechanism, which is breathtakingly simple and elegant.

He applied the fundamental principles of design when devising the Cube. He aimed to make each piece as simple and compact as possible, and has said the shapes of pebbles in the Danube inspired him. Rubik believed form follows function, and he was particularly pleased with the spring-loaded screws, which provide the tension that holds the Cube together.

Once he had a working cube, it took him a month to work out a solution method. He has stated that he never wrote anything down—he did it all in his head! He was granted a Hungarian patent on December 31, 1977, and the Politechnika Co-operative agreed to manufacture it, starting in 1977. The rest, as they say, is history.

At the time, Rubik lived in a hilly suburb of Buda in a house he built with his own hands, which is literally on top of his parents' house. In early 1980, Rubik came to London to improve his English, and I met him. I wrote the following description of him in late 1981: "He is initially reserved but

ERNŐ RUBIK

ORIGINAL HUNGARIAN PACKAGE FOR
THE CUBE, AUTOGRAPHED BY RUBIK

MAGIC CUBE PACKAGE BY LOGICAL GAMES

opens up when the conversation gets into three dimensions. His conversation and manner are serious and intense. He often replies in a way, which opens up more questions and thoughts to consider. He is one of the few people that I have met who soon comes across as a genius."

THE CUBE SPREADS

The Cube was initially called The Magic Cube, *Büvös Kocka* in Hungarian, and *Zauber Würfel* in German. It was some months before we learned the inventor's name, and the initial report actually said he was dead. Politechnika did an initial production run of 5,000 in early 1977. That fall, they decided to launch an advertising campaign to sell them for Christmas. Somebody thought to check with the warehouse and discovered the stock had already sold out.

The Cube won a prize at the Budapest International Fair in 1978, which led to foreign orders. Production was stepped up and trucks were driving to Hungary from all over Europe and filling up with Cubes. In 1979, Rubik received a prize from the Hungarian Ministry of Education and Culture. The Cube also received Toy of the Year awards for 1981 in the U.K., France, and Germany. It won the U.K. Toy of the

Year award again in 1982, the only product to win two years in a row. In 1990, Rubik was elected president of the Hungarian Engineering Academy.

My connection with the Cube began in the summer of 1978, at the International Congress of Mathematicians in Helsinki, when I heard that some people had this new cubical puzzle from Hungary. In particular, John Conway (then at Cambridge; now at Princeton) and Roger Penrose (now Sir Roger, at Oxford) had samples. Penrose had a pocket full of diagrams to solve the puzzle on backs of envelopes, and Conway could solve the Cube, without consulting notes, in under four minutes! I obtained my first Cube from Tamás Varga, Hungary's leading mathematical educator, who brought a bag of Cubes to the Congress. After playing with it for an entire night and seeing others do the same, I knew this was something special.

When I got home, my wife recognized the Cube as an enemy as soon as I showed it to her.

I made inquiries to the Hungarian Consulate about importing Cubes to the U.K. I also got in touch with Hungarians who kindly sent me small packets of six to twelve Cubes. When these arrived, my departmental colleagues hovered near the boxes, reminding me that I had promised them one.

In December 1978, I received a letter from a Hungarian importer saying he had received "a quantity" of the Cubes. I called him and asked for sixty. These were sold in the few minutes it took me to walk around my department, so I called back and increased the order to a hundred. By the end of the week, I ordered two hundred more, and the numbers increased from then on. The importer had five thousand Cubes, which he thought would last a year. I sold them in about three months.

Until we had started getting reasonable supplies of the Cube, we treated the devices with great care. No one dared to take one apart, so the mechanism remained a mystery. A neighbor of mine was the first person I knew who dared to disassemble the Cube. He found that when you peeled the sticker off a center piece, a lid was exposed. A little prying with a small screwdriver or knife lifted this lid to reveal a spring-loaded screw inside. This easily unscrewed, and the entire cube could be taken to pieces. There's an easier way to take it apart—rotate one face by 45 degrees and then lift an edge piece in that face.

Once you get one edge out, the rest of the Cube easily comes to pieces, and you can appreciate the elegant simplicity of the mechanism. The center pieces of each face

TAKING A CUBE APART REVEALS RUBIK'S ELEGANT MECHANISM

are attached to a central spindle by screws. The edge pieces rotate under the face centers, and the corners rotate under the edges. In order to rotate smoothly, there has to be a little give in the mechanism, and this is provided by having the spring-loaded screws, which also take up some wear.

If you take the Cube apart, be sure to reassemble it in its solved state. A randomly assembled Cube has only a one in twelve chance of ever being solved. I have heard of people sneaking into colleagues' homes or offices and taking Cubes apart and reassembling them incorrectly, driving the owners mad. Of course, you could also peel off some of the stickers and rearrange them.

God's Algorithm

There are two methods to count moves: by faces and by quarter turns. The difference is that a 180 degree turn of a face is counted as one face move, but as two quarter turns. I originally adopted the face count as it seemed to measure the effort of the solution better than the quarter-turn count.

As of September 2008, the lower limit is 20 moves and the upper limit is 22, both counting face moves. A position requiring 20 moves was found by Dik T. Winter in 1992 and shown not to be solvable in fewer moves by Michael Reid in 1995. The upper bound is due to Tomas Rokicki in August 2008, but his searching has not turned up any position requiring 21 or 22 moves.

Solving the Cube

In Helsinki and back in London, I became increasingly interested in "solving" the Cube (restoring it to the initial position from any random position). I recall lying awake several nights and, about two weeks after getting home, finally seeing that one could move any four edge pieces into a given set of edge positions and the rest of the solution would follow easily. It wasn't an elegant solution, but it worked.

The Cube has 43,252,003,274,489, 856,000 possible positions (that's 43 quintillions and change—I think I was the first to multiply this out to get the full 20 digits). If the faces of the Cube have pictures rather than just colors (as some versions do), you have to multiply this number by 2,048 to come up with the number of possible positions.

John Conway, one of the world's greatest group theorists, observed that the Cube obeys what are known as conservation (or parity) laws, meaning that some moves are simply not possible. Either Conway or one of his colleagues at Cambridge defined the shortest route from any given position back to the starting position as "God's Algorithm."

I noticed that everybody who was discussing solutions was using their own notation, usually based on x, y, z, and usually failing to explain it clearly. It was often unclear which way their basic turns went, especially for the faces behind the cube. This led me to write up my own method. I made around 30 copies of this handwritten method, using a notation avoiding x, y, z, but still basically mathematical (I cannot locate a copy of this paper—if you have one, please send me a copy). Conway also had a notation, but it was a bit whimsical and ultimately based on the colors on his cube. At the time, the color pattern was not standardized. A neighbor told me about his son trying to tell a friend how to solve his cube over the telephone: "Now turn the red face—that's blue on your cube. Then turn the green face—that's yellow on your cube…."

I realized that a notation needed to avoid colors and be simple enough for anyone to know where the directions were. I came up with using the directions Front, Back, Left, Right, Up, and Down. I recall wanting to use Top and Bottom, but rejecting these because I already had a B (Back). The notation provides a simple way to name faces and pieces of the Cube and to name movements of the faces. I standardized the movements by using a letter, such as B, to denote a clockwise movement of the Back face—as viewed when looking at the Back face.

I wrote up a manuscript solution method in this notation, and copies were made in February 1979. It was titled *Notes on the 'Magic Cube'* because the name "Rubik's Cube™" was not adopted until 1980. The notation rapidly replaced all other notations and helped make the subsequent proliferation of work on the Cube possible. Of all my work, it may be the most likely to survive. Material and ideas continued to arrive faster than I could deal with, and the *Notes* were eventually expanded to 75 pages in August 1980. The last version included a four-page section: "A Step by Step Solution of Rubik's 'Magic Cube,'" which sold more than fifty thousand copies. I then started a *Cubic Circular*, which ran to eight issues from 1981 to 1985. It can now be found on the Internet.

Suzanne Lowry, woman's editor of *The Observer*, asked me to write an article on the Cube. It appeared as "Six-sided Magic" on June 17, 1979, and may have been the first article on the Cube outside Hungary. I also wrote an article called "The Hungarian Magic Cube" for *The Mathematical Intelligencer* in 1979, which helped spread basic information about the Cube and its mathematics throughout the mathematical world.

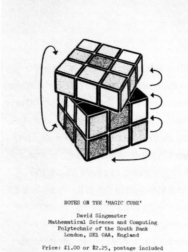

NOTES ON THE 'MAGIC CUBE'

David Singmaster
Mathematical Sciences and Computing
Polytechnic of the South Bank
London, SE1 0AA, England

Price: £1.00 or $2.25, postage included

SINGMASTER'S NOTES, 1979

CUBIC CIRCULAR, 1981

THE WORLD GOES CUBE CRAZY

Tibor Laczi, a Hungarian-born businessman who worked for a major German computer manufacturer, "discovered" the Cube in a café while driving to Budapest on a business trip in 1978. His waiter had the puzzle but didn't know how to solve it. Laczi saw its potential immediately and bought it from him for $1.

After meeting with Rubik, Laczi brought the Cube to the Nuremberg Toy Fair in February 1979 hoping to find a potential German toy distributor. There he met toy developer Tom Kremer, a native Hungarian who ran the London-based licensing company Seven Towns Ltd. Kremer was fascinated by the Cube and agreed to help Laczi translate the Hungarian success of the Cube to the world stage.

Cube Myths

As the Cube's popularity spread, so did its aura of mystery. Legend has it that one of John Conway's graduate students got his beard or tie caught in a Cube and it slowly pulled him into the puzzle. Conway's group figured he would reappear when the Cube was returned to the same position it was in when he was first trapped. But no one remembered what it was, and, as the story goes, the missing cubist was never seen again. It seems appropriate that a German advertisement for the Cube once stated: "Do not take hold of it—it will not let you go."

RUBIK'S CUBE™

Laczi headed back to Hungary to pave the way with the prevailing Hungarian bureaucracy, while Tom Kremer set off on a world tour of toy manufacturers. Unfortunately he found that none of the leading players in the field shared their enthusiasm. Although impressed by the Cube, the general view within the industry estimated its prospects to be poor. Its "faults" were numerous: too difficult and expensive to manufacture; impossible to demonstrate its fascination on TV; too abstract; too cerebral; too quiet; a challenge for the esoteric academic mind rather than a puzzle meant for children and the general public.

After many disappointments, Kremer persuaded Stewart Sims, vice president of marketing at the Ideal Toy Corporation, to come to Hungary and see the Cube in play. It was now September 1979, and the Cube could occasionally be seen on Hungarian streets, trams, and in cafés. After days of negotiations between communist Hungary and capitalist America, and Kremer and Laczi furiously mediating between the two, Ideal Toy was sold one million Cubes and exclusive rights to the Magic Cube.

So, in late 1979, Ideal took over the distribution of the Cube. Reportedly, they paid Konsumex a million dollars advance. Ideal didn't like the "Magic" part of the name—they thought some might associate magic with evil spirits—and wanted to rename it. Both Gordian Knot and Inca Gold had been suggested as names, but Sims didn't like them, and they would have

been difficult to copyright. "Rubik's Cube™" came to him after a few days. It has a pleasant assonance and could be legally protected, which was important since Rubik had patented the Cube only in Hungary. At the time, I knew of no other toy named for its inventor. In 1981, the name Rubik's Cube™ was entered in the *Oxford English Dictionary* and the Brockhaus *Lexicon*. U.K. Customs even introduced a new category for it: Rubik's Cube™ and the like.

Politechnika changed their name to Politoys and improved their production on the Cube. The resulting puzzle was lighter, smoother in finish, and much easier to turn. Ideal's promotion of the Cube in the U.S. started with a party given by Hungarian Zsa Zsa Gabor in Beverly Hills on May 5, 1980.

Ideal packaged the Cube in clear plastic cylinders in order to increase the visibility of the product. Their retail price in the U.K. (around £6 or £7) was about twice what I and other puzzle sellers in the U.K. had been charging. Nonetheless, Ideal sold about four and a half million Cubes in 1980 and anticipated U.S. sales of about ten million in 1981. I've estimated they sold perhaps twenty million by the fall of that year. The Taiwanese reportedly sold about three times as many. There were reports of a Munich shop selling eight hundred Cubes in an hour and of a Wolverhampton (U.K.) shop selling two thousand in an hour. Market traders sold a thousand easily on a Saturday.

The Cube was Hungary's biggest single earner of foreign currency. By 1981, there were reports that Rubik was the richest man in Hungary.

In February 1979, I gave my first lecture on the Cube, at the University of Exeter. Within a few years, I had given about seventy lectures in nine countries. In December 1979, I went to New York and presented a Cube to Martin Gardner, which led to a cover story about the Cube in *Scientific American* by Douglas Hofstadter in March 1981.

Clubs and Newsletters

During 1980, a computer bulletin board, called Cube-lovers, was started at MIT. When this closed in 1996, it was one of the longest-running bulletin boards on the Internet. By the fall of 1981, I knew of eight Cube clubs worldwide, and there were probably many more. Since then, many other clubs have come and mostly gone.

Anneke Treep and Just van Rossum founded the only Cube club organization that is still very active. It began in 1981 as a Dutch-language newsletter and evolved into the Nederlandse Kubus Club (Dutch Cubists' Club). The club's quarterly newsletter, *Cubism for Fun*, published in English for many years, is still going strong after almost thirty years. It now covers puzzles in general, and they hold an annual Cube Day gathering of puzzle lovers.

Cube Challenges

A colleague of mine, Paul Taylor, was walking in the South Downs, England, during Easter of 1980 and found a Cube in a pub. The pub offered a bottle of whiskey to anyone who could restore the Cube. It took him a while, but when he solved it, the landlord accused him of cheating and refused to pay up.

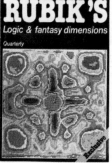 

RUBIK'S CUBE NEWSLETTER, BASED NEAR NEW YORK, STARTED IN MAY 1981. FOUR ISSUES WERE PUBLISHED.

RUBIK'S—LOGIC AND FANTASY DIMENSIONS STARTED IN 1982. EIGHT ISSUES WERE PUBLISHED.

CUBISM FOR FUN, ISSUE #14, MARCH 1987

Fastest Times

Single times for solving a Cube are not a good measure of ability, but they are fascinating and amusing to record. Here are some earliest fast times that are known.

- In the summer of 1978, John Conway could solve the Cube in less than four minutes—at the time, we knew nobody else who could do it without notes.

- Perhaps the earliest Cube competitions were those organized by Kate Fried in Budapest in early 1980. Solving times of 55, 40, 46, and 36 seconds were reported in early 1980.

- In my *Notes*, the shortest known time was credited to Nicolas Hammond, with 36 seconds. He did it in 37 seconds on BBC TV on January 24, 1981. By late 1981, Hammond achieved 28 seconds—he was 17 at the time.

- In Hamburg, Germany, 16-year-old Ronald Brinkmann solved the Cube in 29 seconds on German TV and later reached 24 seconds. When asked for advice, Brinkmann replied, "Turn, turn, turn."

- In Paris, Jérôme Jean-Charles, 25, worked on efficient solving, achieving an average of 36 seconds, then 32 seconds, with a minimum of 21 seconds. He could do up to 180 moves per minute and a 126-move process in 37 seconds.

- In Liverpool, 16-year-old Michael Musker was timed at 20 seconds and said he once solved the Cube in 14 seconds when no one was watching.

- In Australia, 21-year-old Geoff Harris claimed he solved a cube in 7 seconds!

At this point, the problem of determining whether the Cube was really in a random position became apparent—even I can solve some positions in one or two moves, which takes only a few seconds. Although any five or six moves effectively randomizes the Cube, some random positions are much closer to a solved state than others, and this varies depending on the algorithm used by the solver. Therefore, it is quite unreasonable to take single times. The solver should have several trials, and the Cubes should be identical patterns for each person. Even then, as in all sporting events, luck will still play some role.

THE BRITISH CHAMPIONSHIPS IN 1981

Competitions

Throughout 1981, there were many competitions, and Ideal began organizing a World Championship, with regional champions going to national championships. The U.K. finals were held in December 1981 in London. The contestants picked new Cubes, which had been randomized by a computer, from a bin. Julian Chilvers, 15, from Norwich, won the U.K. Championship. He clocked 25.79 seconds, a world record, on his third trial and had the second-best time, 28.36 seconds, on the second trial. He reported that he used ordinary car grease as a lubricant. Another said he didn't like Vaseline as it ran out when his Cube "got hot." One contestant had

sweatbands on his arms, but he confessed it was mostly to frighten the opposition. Nial Ferguson, the Irish champion, was, at 20, the oldest competitor. He wore gloves between trials to keep his hands warm.

Other impressive Cube feats:

- Jérôme Jean-Charles won the French national finals with a time of 25.6 seconds.

- The New England regional was won by a 9-year-old named Jonathan Cheyer in 48.31 seconds.

- John White, 19, a second-year mathematics student at the University of Warwick, could do the Cube behind his back after 10 minutes of study.

- Rainer Seitz reported that a boy in Germany could do two cubes at once—one in each hand.

- Mal Davies reported that Richard Hodson, of Queen Mary's Grammar School, Walsall, could do a Cube one-handed in 89 seconds.

The U.S. Championship was recorded for the TV show, *That's Incredible*, on November 13, 1981, and broadcast on December 7. Minh Thai, a 16-year-old student, won with a time of 26.04 seconds. The first prize was $2,000 plus a trip to the World Championships. Second place went to Jeffrey Varasano, with a time of 28.96

JOHN WHITE SOLVING THE CUBE BEHIND HIS BACK

RICHARD HODSON SOLVES A CUBE ONE-HANDED

seconds. Jeffrey held the U.S. record with a time of 24.67 seconds in the Eastern Regional Competition.

The first Rubik's Cube™ World Championship was held in Budapest on June 5, 1982, and was sponsored by Politoys, Konsumex, and Ideal. There were contestants

THE COMPETITORS AT THE FIRST RUBIK'S CUBE™ WORLD CHAMPIONSHIP

from 19 countries, ranging from 14 to 26 years old. The competition was organized by the public relations firm for Ideal (U.K.), so it had the same basic structure as the U.K. contest. The Cubes were selected by Rubik from a special production run, and competitors were given a sample to practice with. All had a standardized color pattern, with white opposite yellow, red opposite orange, and blue opposite green,

and with blue, orange, and yellow clockwise at a corner (spelling BOY).

Rubik worked with mathematicians to develop several patterns of similar complexity for the Cubes. Four sets of Cubes were put in four of these patterns by Rubik and sealed in separate briefcases, which were kept in a bank overnight and brought to the competition by the supervising lawyer. One case was opened and placed by the competitors' entrance. The competitors remained offstage until their turn so they could not watch the previous attempts. Each contestant picked one Cube at random as he came on stage and had three attempts, of which the best time was taken. The fourth cube was used as an alternate in case a cube came apart.

When his turn came, the contestant had fifteen seconds to examine the Cube in his hand. It was then set down on a photoelectric base. Time began when the contestant picked up the Cube again and stopped when it was set down again in completed form.

Minh Thai was the winner, with a best time of 22.95 seconds. He was a 16-year-old from Los Angeles who had come to the U.S. three years earlier from Vietnam, speaking no English. Seven days after buying the Cube, he could solve it in less than two minutes.

Trophies for the championship were Cubes that had one corner replaced by a globe—which was also the logo of the contest—plated in gold, silver, and bronze.

At the end of the championship, Ideal gave the participants samples of their new larger cube, the 4×4×4 "Rubik's Revenge." Many of us worked on it on the flight out of Budapest, and I was pleased to solve mine before Minh Thai did. I later realized this was due more to luck than skill as there can be an extra glitch in the 4×4×4, which does not occur in the 3×3×3, and it happened that this did not occur when I was solving it.

In 2003, as the Cube began to resurface, Dan Gosbee organized the second World Championship in Toronto. Since then, there have been many Cube competitions, covering the whole range of Cubes: 2×2×2, 3×3×3, 4×4×4, 5×5×5, and other Rubik products. These are now governed by the World Cube Association. The current revival of interest in the Cube led to 72 official competitions between 2003 and 2006. These use a best average time, taking five trials and averaging the three middle times, recorded by a special timer. They also record best single times. A Canadian software engineer, Dan Knights, won the 3×3×3 event in 2003 with an average of 20.00 seconds.

At the time of this printing, the world record for a single time was 7.08 seconds, set by Erik Akkersdijk at the Czech Open 2008. The world record average solution is 11.28 seconds by Yu Nakajima at the Kashiwa Open, May 4, 2008. The 4×4×4 has been solved in 41.16 seconds, the 5×5×5 has been solved in 1 minute 16.21 seconds, and the 2×2×2 has been solved in .96 seconds.

A HUNGARIAN STAMP WAS ISSUED FOR THE WORLD CHAMPIONSHIP

Fun Cube Facts

- A football game in Connecticut was delayed due to a missing player who was discovered playing with his Cube in the locker room.

- Two people followed Robert Cole, a colleague of mine, out of a waiting room into his train compartment when he was playing with his Cube. Fifteen minutes later, one of them realized he was on the wrong train.

- English Cube mania began when Rubik appeared on *Swap-Shop*, a Saturday morning BBC TV children's program, on January 24, 1981, with Nicolas Hammond, who solved the Cube in 37 seconds. The competing show, on ITV, *Tiswas*, then launched a "Stamp Out Cubes" campaign.

- Several different variations of cubes for the blind were created.

CUBES FOR THE BLIND

- Rubik's Cube™ has become a household word—it has been used as a metaphor in political, educational, and economic contexts as well as in numerous cartoons:

1. The first political cartoon was created by Felix Mussil in *Frankfurter Rundschau* in 1981 showing a bemused Chancellor Helmut Schmidt with a Cube labeled "Berlin, unemployment."

2. On July 7, 1981, Nicholas Garland published a cartoon in *The Daily Telegraph* showing Willie Whitelaw and Maggie Thatcher struggling with a Cube labeled "racial violence."

3. A Mahood cartoon in *Punch* printed in 1981 shows "The Russian Cube"—an enormous Cube being parachuted onto troops—"A variation of the Rubik Cube, this game is guaranteed to drive any enemy to distraction within minutes."

NICHOLAS GARLAND'S CARTOON FROM *THE DAILY TELEGRAPH*

THE 1981 MAHOOD CARTOON IN *PUNCH*

CHANCELLOR SCHMIDT ON THE COVER OF *STERN* MAGAZINE IN 1981

- One man wrote that the Cube has allowed him to come out of the closet—the mathematical closet, that is. In the past, when he told people he was a mathematician, they treated him like a social outcast. Now they ask how to do the Cube.

- Solomon Golomb devised an analogy between Cube corners and quarks, which he has extended into a complete Cubic cosmology.

- Rubik's Cube™ has been placed in the design section of the Museum of Modern Art in New York City.

- The Cube has even inspired music.

1. "Mr. Rubik" by the Barron Knights appeared on their LP *Twisting the Knights Away* and was available in 1981.

2. A Hungarian husband and wife, Bea Muszty and András Dobay, wrote the single "Trick in the Middle" in 1982.

3. The renowned inventor of information theory and error-correcting codes, Claude Shannon, wrote an extraordinary song about the Cube called "A Rubric on Rubik Cubics." His later version appeared in my *Cubic Circular* and his *Collected Works*.

"MR. RUBIK," BY THE BARRON KNIGHTS

"TRICK IN THE MIDDLE," WRITTEN BY BEA MUSZTY AND ANDRÁS DOBAY

Books on the Cube

In 1981, Rubik and several colleagues wrote the book *A Büvös Kocka (The Magic Cube)*. I wrote the foreword, called "The Fascination of Rubik's Cube™," and I later edited an English translation, which was released in 1987 as *Rubik's Cubic Compendium*, in the Recreations in Mathematics Series that I edited for Oxford University Press.

In this book, Rubik analyzed the features of the Cube that made it unique: the pieces stay together; more than one piece moves at a time; and the pieces have orientation as well as position.

Since then, many other puzzles with these properties have appeared, but the generic term for these tends to be "Rubik's Cube™ and similar puzzles."

There were many books about the Rubik's Cube™ and how to solve it. One count based on the bibliography of Georges Helm gives the following numbers of books in each of the following years of the Cube craze: 14 (1979); 52 (1980); 174 (1981); 70 (1982); and 15 (1983).

Rubik's Cube™ solution books topped *The New York Times* best-seller list for 40 weeks straight beginning on July 12, 1981. Three of the books occupied the top position: James G. Nourse's *The Simple Solution to Rubik's Cube™*; Australian Don Taylor's *Mastering Rubik's Cube™* and *You Can Do the Cube*, written by 13-year-old Patrick Bossert. On January 24, 1982, Nourse was at the top of the mass-market list, with his second book at sixth, while Bossert and Taylor were first and second on the trade list, and books by Østrup and Taylor & Rylands were at positions 9 and 12. Based on solution book sales, this date was likely the peak of the Rubik's Cube™ craze. Nourse was on the list for 34 weeks and Taylor was on the list for 38 weeks. Bossert's book sold well over a million copies, possibly three million, and Nourse sold over six million!

Side Effects of the Cube

The early cubes were very stiff, and the solver tended to grip it firmly in the left hand, pressing on the tendon of the left thumb. This could lead to an inflammation known as Cubist's Thumb. If the person was older than about 50, when the tendon-sheath lubrication would decline, the inflammation might require a small operation. Cubist's Thumb is apparently the same as Disco Digit; which made it into the *New England Journal of Medicine* in 1981.

When I was working on my book, I was constantly checking processes, and I began to get what I called Rubik's Wrist, rather like the repetitive strain injury associated with excessive terminal use.

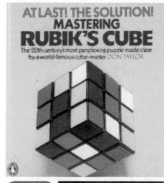

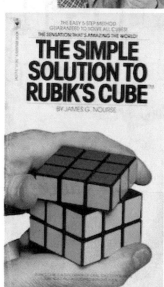

DON TAYLOR'S BOOK WAS ONE OF THE MOST POPULAR CUBE BOOKS IN THE 1980s

PATRICK BOSSERT WAS 13 YEARS OLD WHEN HE WROTE HIS BEST-SELLING BOOK

NOURSE'S BOOK SOLD OVER SIX MILLION COPIES

On the positive side, Eric Pfisterer of Toronto reported that the Cube cured his tennis elbow. My tennis-playing friends thought this must be because he stopped playing tennis for so long, but he replied that similar hand exercises are standard treatment for the condition.

The Rubik's Cube™ was banned from Bath High School as a safety hazard. "[Students] bump into each other and fall over objects while concentrating on the Cubes," said Headmistress Doris Chapman. Rubik's Cubes™ were banned at Wandsworth Prison, London, after one was found stuffed with cannabis.

I met a doctor who worked in a teenage leukemia ward who said there was a pressing need to distract the teenage patients. The Cube was the best distraction he ever had.

A mother wrote to the *Daily Express* that her 14-year-old daughter, who is severely handicapped, has learned how to do the Cube—much to her delight and the amazement of the rest of the family.

Henry Ernest Dudeney, writing about the craze produced by the 15 Puzzle in 1873, said, "It has been stated, though doubtless it was a Yankee exaggeration, that some 1,500 weak-minded persons in America alone were driven to insanity by it." My business partner, Jane Nankivell, suggested the following slogan for use on our shirts: "Rubik's Cube™ Cures Sanity." Fortunately, we have not yet heard of any real cases.

CUBE T-SHIRT

The Trials of the Cube

Ideal Toys and Politoys commenced legal action against Taiwanese knock-off Cubes early in 1981. The first case to reach court in the U.K. was against London-based Dallas Print Transfers and Dallas Marketing for their Wonderful Puzzler. There were two grounds—infringement of copyright and "passing off," which means selling an imitation product similar to an established original so as to mislead the public. The infringement of copyright was established and the judgment was upheld.

However, despite the fact that Dallas's product was identical to the Rubik product in size, coloring, and even the cylindrical plastic package, Ideal was not victorious on the grounds of "passing off." Ideal was held not to have established that they had created a brand image, due to the pre-1980 sales and the lack of image promotion. However, due to the lawsuit the whole Dallas operation went bankrupt.

Ideal then pursued all toy stores that had sold pirate cubes. Almost all the shops had to sign consent orders agreeing not to ever sell pirate cubes again. Ideal's chief counsel described stakeouts in the back streets of Tilbury (the container port of London), which led to seizures of containers of pirate cubes in the middle of the night.

In the U.S., Ideal obtained several injunctions and attempted to block the importation of pirate cubes. A major importer of these pirate cubes claimed that he bought the puzzles from the factories that made them for Ideal, but this was never proven.

According to Seven Towns Ltd, the Cube continues to be protected by over 60 trademarks worldwide, which protect not only the puzzle but also the use of its image in TV, film, and advertising. Customs officials regularly seize unauthorized cubes, which are subsequently destroyed. In 2007, over 500,000 counterfeit cubes were destroyed worldwide.

THE CRAZE RUNS DOWN... AND COMES BACK

Cube Backlash

As with any craze, interest waned. There were some contributory factors. In early 1981, demand had so outstripped production that there was a Cube famine. The high price charged by Ideal led to the production of imitations in the Far East, notably in Taiwan, Hong Kong, and Korea, where copyright and patent enforcement was still minimal. During the great Cube famine of early 1981, I heard of a second-hand Cube market and offers of £15 for a Cube. Pirate cubes began to flood the market and were being sold on the streets for less than Ideal's wholesale price. Despite the imitations being less smooth and less sturdy than the Ideal Cubes, pirates probably sold about three times as many as Ideal. The fact that pirate cubes were selling for less than the wholesale price caused many major shops to stop selling or stocking Cubes, or any other puzzle, leading to a major recession in the puzzle market.

FRUSTRATED SOLVERS COVERED THEIR CUBES IN STICKERS SO THEY APPEARED TO BE SOLVED

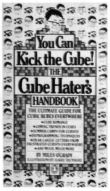

THE CUBE BACKLASH INCLUDED SEVERAL BOOKS

By 1982, a Rubik's Cube™ backlash had begun. Stickers appeared that could be used to make people think the Cube had been solved. Around that time, single-color cubes were marketed as novelty items. Many color variations appeared, including the Irish Cube, with all green faces, and the Aggie Puzzle (presumably a reference to Texas A&M University), with all red faces. There were even solid brass cubes.

Other novelty items such as coffee mugs and statuettes mocking the Cube followed. One favorite showed a slightly melted cube, transfixed by a large brass screw, mounted on a wood base with a brass plate that read "SCREW IT." Then a Cube Smasher was marketed—it was just a mallet with a label.

Numerous humorous books appeared poking fun at the Cube solver and the earlier Cube books. The various magazines and clubs ceased or wound down—only the Dutch Cubist's Club survived.

Resurgence of the Cube

The number of Cubes sold worldwide is unknown. Various people, including some at Seven Towns, have estimated sales of the Cube are over 300 million worldwide.

By the end of 1983, the Rubik's Cube™ craze was over.

However, it appears the Cube is having a second life. The puzzles have been popping up at toy stores, at bookstores, and on the Internet over the last five years. Access to solutions, the growth of speed-cubing groups, and marketing by the distributors of the Cube has once again made it a must-have puzzle. In recent years strong growth has been reported in such regions as Russia, India, and the Far East, where genuine Rubik's Cubes™ had once been hard to purchase. Other signs of a resurgence in rotational puzzles are the large number of speed solving contests worldwide, the new production of 6×6×6 and 7×7×7 V-CUBE™S, and many amazing new handmade rotational puzzles being designed and fabricated, with quite a few of the most creative ones being produced under license.

A good puzzle often becomes very popular and then wanes, but it returns as a perennial favorite. In 1904, Henry Dudeney, a leading creator of puzzles at the time, described the 15 Puzzle "as dead as Queen Anne," but you can buy dozens of versions of the puzzle today. In the 1980s, I said that the Cube would become one of the standard puzzles for all future generations, and this seems to be coming true.

6×6×6 AND 7×7×7 V-CUBE™S

Chapter 3

Puzzles Inspired by the Rubik's Cube ™

By Geert Hellings

BŰVÖS KOCKA

Politechnika IPARI SZÖVETKEZET

térbeli logikai játék

RUBIK'S CUBE™ IN
HUNGARIAN PACKAGING

MORE CUBE PUZZLES

3×3×3 Variations

Modified versions of the Rubik's Cube™ were produced soon after the introduction of the original puzzle. They were initially manufactured by companies in Taiwan and later in Japanese and Russian firms. The new shapes included the Octagonal Barrel, Ball, Truncated Cube (a shape of six octagonal faces and eight triangular faces), Cuboctahedron (a shape of eight triangular faces and six square faces), Million Space Shuttle (also called Cushion or Pillow), Russian Missing Edges Cube, Diamond Puzzle, and Rhombic Dodecahedron. Rubik's first wooden prototype was actually not a cube, but a truncated cube.

OCTAGONAL BARREL

BALL

TRUNCATED CUBE

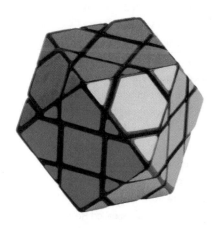

CUBOCTAHEDRON

MILLION SPACE SHUTTLE
(ALSO CALLED CUSHION OR PILLOW)

RUSSIAN MISSING EDGES CUBE

DIAMOND PUZZLE

RHOMBIC DODECAHEDRON

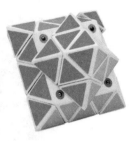

Another version of the 3×3×3 is the octahedron, which consists of eight equilateral triangles, four of which meet at each vertex. The puzzle looks complex, but it actually uses a 3×3×3 mechanism similar to the original Cube. If you ignore the ornamental rotating tips, the Magic Octahedron can only rotate and exchange parts on 3 planes. One version, the Trajber's Octahedron was produced in Taiwan. Truncated versions of the octahedron puzzle are Christoph's Magic Jewel and the Russian Magic Jewel, a souvenir from Penza, Russia.

2×2×2 Variations

After the 3×3×3 Cube became so popular, Ernő Rubik applied for and received a patent for the 2×2×2 Pocket Cube in 1983. Other mechanisms for the 2×2×2 Cube have been patented and produced by several companies, including a version by the Taiwan company Eastsheen. Although the number of possible positions for the 2×2×2 is only 3,674,160 and it can be solved in a maximum of 11 moves, it can be surprisingly difficult to solve.

One variation of the 2×2×2 Cube are 2×2×2 balls, which were made by several firms and display different sizes and colors. Saleh Khoudary patented the K-Ball in 2000, and a cylindrical version, called Rota, was manufactured by Swiss toy maker Naef in several color variations. Truncating the corners of a 2×2×2 Cube creates an octahedron, but the simple coloring of the faces makes for a trivial puzzle, so colored dots were placed on the tips. The resulting product was named Okki, Polka-Diamond, or Gem, which was produced in East Germany by VEB Spielwaren.

FROM LEFT:
POCKET CUBE
K-BALL
ROTA
OKKI, POLKA-DIAMOND, OR GEM

By adding four tetrahedron tips to the Okki puzzle, a tetrahedron shape is created. A tetrahedron is made of four triangular faces, three of which meet at each vertex. Two examples of this are the Pyramorphix, created by Uwe Meffert, and the Figurenmatch, which was made in Germany. Adding another four tetrahedron tips results in the Star Puzzle, which was created in East Germany along with the East German House puzzle. The latter was created by truncating the edges of a 2×2×2 Cube.

Since the mechanical construction of the 2×2×2 puzzle is relatively simple, it lent itself to some interesting—and marketable—shapes. There are more than 50 of these customized puzzles. Many of them were only available for a very short time. Some were used as giveaways at fast-food restaurants, and others were enclosed in cereal packages.

Both 2×2×2 and 3×3×3 mechanisms have been used to produce puzzles in the shape of the globe. A special 2×2×2 version is the Korean Cosmos puzzle produced by Dyne, which has additional circular elements at the intersections that can be turned independently using an outside piece.

A similar, but larger, circular mechanism is found in the Spanish Marusenko puzzle that was introduced in 2008. The inventors of this puzzle are Félix-Abdon Pérez Cabeza and Aleksandr Marusenko.

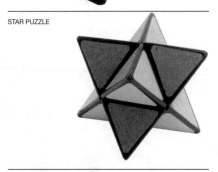

PYRAMORPHIX

STAR PUZZLE

EAST GERMAN HOUSE

MORPH 1×2×2 PUZZLE

MARUSENKO

RUBIK'S WORLD

KOREAN COSMOS

GLOBE

Ernő Rubik invented a 2×3×3 puzzle, called the Magic Domino, which was mass-produced in Hungary in the early 1980s. The original Magic Dominos were made out of nine white and nine black cubes, covered with domino dots, and they have 410 million positions. Both spindle mechanisms and grooved mechanisms were manufactured, as well as a Russian version with a different mechanism. As a result of the success of the Magic Domino puzzle, various smaller knock off variations were produced in Taiwan, with red-and-white or black-and-white design patterns.

MAGIC DOMINO

MARVEL DOMINO

The 4×4×4

Peter Sebestény, a mathematician from Budapest, invented the 4×4×4 cube in 1980. He had taken some 3×3×3 cubes to Hamburg, Germany, and found that the puzzles were not yet available there. While in Budapest, he figured out his own solution to the 3×3×3 cube and could solve it in 3 to 3.5 minutes. He was looking for a way to earn a living in Hamburg when some friends suggested that he design a 4×4×4 cube. It took him two months to do all the calculations, work out all the details, and make drawings of his design. His main idea

was to split the center axis of the 3×3×3 into four parts and let the parts rotate freely around a core. They were held in place by shield-shaped pieces. These center parts hold the edge and corner pieces, preventing the cube from falling apart.

However, during the design process, he was faced with several problems. The main problem was that a completely symmetric and freely moving core of the cube could remain in an undefined position somewhere halfway down between two half cubes when you tried to rotate half of the cube. This could make the next half-half turn that is perpendicular to the last rotation impossible, because the core could obstruct the movement. The solution to this problem led to his introduction of a blocking system of several spherical

PETER SEBESTÉNY

PETER SEBESTÉNY'S
4×4×4 CUBE

5×5×5 CUBE

JÜRGEN HOFFMAN MADE A BRASS 5X5X5 CUBE
IN 1981, BUT IT WAS NEVER PATENTED.

triangles. These ensure that the core always moves along with one half of the cube when the half sides are rotated.

Initially, Sebestény designed the 4×4×4 cube with cubies the same size as the successful 3×3×3 cube, but he found that this made the puzzle too big. He decided on a 66 mm edge length, created a prototype, and was granted a patent on December 20, 1983. He first planned to name the 4×4×4 cube "Sebestény's Cube," but he later decided to let it be a Rubik's Cube™. He felt that "without the 3×3×3, there would not be a 4×4×4; my cube was only the next logical step following Professor Rubik's ingenious concept." The 4×4×4 cube was introduced onto the market in 1982 by Ideal Company with the product names Rubik's Revenge in the U.S. and Rubik's Master Cube in Europe. Now it is called Rubik's 4×4×4 Cube in the U.S. The production of these cubes by Ideal was stopped after a couple of years during the market downturn but was later restarted by Uwe Meffert. In 2002, Eastsheen introduced a new 4×4×4 cube using a different mechanism. The number of possible positions of the 4×4×4 is 7.4×10^{45}.

The 5×5×5

Udo Krell, who also lived in Hamburg, invented the 5×5×5 cube in 1986. It was initially marketed in Germany and called Rubik's *Wahn* (Illusion) and later was changed to the Professor Cube, and now it is called the Rubik's 5×5×5 Cube in the U.S. The number of possible positions is 2.8×10^{74}. There are other variations of the 5×5×5, including one by Uwe Meffert and another by Eastsheen. The original version by Udo Krell measures 70 mm per edge. The Eastsheen cubes are slightly smaller at 60 mm.

The V-CUBE™S, 5×5×5, 6×6×6, and 7×7×7

For many years, a 6×6×6 cube was considered impossible due to geometry constraints. However, at the 2005 International Puzzle Party in Helsinki, a fully working 6×6×6 V-CUBE™ puzzle was demonstrated by its inventor, Greek engineer Panagiotis Verdes. The puzzle received an Honorable Mention Award at the Puzzle Design Competition during the party.

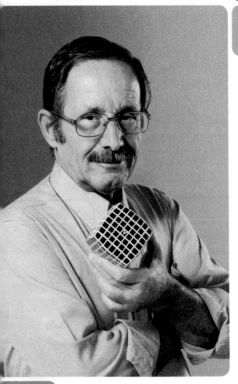

When he first saw the Rubik's Cube™ in 1981, Verdes believed that higher-order cubes with more layers should be possible. Initially, he used the mechanism of the Rubik's Cube™ to try to achieve this, but he soon realized that variations on that mechanism wouldn't solve the problem, especially for the corner cubies. Verdes's unique invention is based on the concept of using concentric, right-angle conical surfaces whose axes of rotation coincide with the semi-axes of the cube. This allows space for the corner pieces to be connected to the inner part of the cube. He created some handmade models in the 1980s, but he kept his ideas to himself. Then, after seeing that the 2×2×2, 4×4×4, and 5×5×5 cubes had been produced, but not the 6×6×6, he decided to apply for a patent for his design. He was awarded one in 2004.

Verdes's patent includes designs for a broad range of rotating cube puzzles from 2×2×2 up to and including the 11×11×11. Higher-order cubes have geometrical constraints and are not considered practical since they would be very expensive and difficult to handle.

The mass-production, marketing, and sales of the V-CUBE™ 5×5×5, V-CUBE™ 6×6×6, and V-CUBE™ 7×7×7 started in the summer of 2008.

The combination of concentric inner spheres and six concentric conical surfaces is a novel principle that is beautifully executed and results in very smooth-turning and reliable puzzles.

The 5×5×5 and 6×6×6 V-CUBE™S are geometric cubes. However, the 7×7×7 puzzle is slightly pillowed in order to preserve its structural integrity. For the same reason, the outer layer of the 6×6×6 V-CUBE™ is slightly wider than the inner layers. The mechanisms of the 6×6×6 and 7×7×7 V-CUBE™S are basically identical. Neglecting the orientation of the black V-sticker, the number of possible positions is 1.57×10^{116} for the 6×6×6 and 1.95×10^{160} for the 7×7×7.

All of the puzzles mentioned in this section were mass-produced, but many of the puzzles introduced in the 1980s are now out of production and not available in shops. They can sometimes be found on eBay or other Web sites. Although subject to change, following is a number of Internet stores that were selling rotational puzzles in 2008:

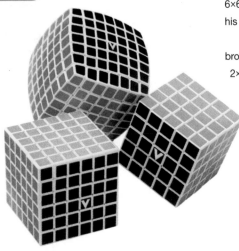

V-CUBE™S, 5×5×5, 6×6×6, AND 7×7×7

9s Puzzles (China): **www.9spuzzles.com**

Cubesmith (USA): **www.cubesmith.com**

Cubikon (Germany): **www.cubikon.de**

Cube4You (China): **www.cube4you.com**

Cubefans (China): **www.cubefans.com**

Hendrik Haak's Puzzle Shop (Germany): **www.puzzle-shop.de**

Meffert (Hong Kong): **www.mefferts.com**

Omega Studio (Taiwan): **www.omega.url.tw/onlineshop**

Puzl.co.uk (United Kingdom): **www.puzl.co.uk**

Puzzlemaster (Canada): **www.puzzlemaster.ca**

Rubiks (USA): **www.rubiks.com**

Rubik's Korea (Korea): **www.rubikskorea.com**

Torito (Japan): **www.torito.jp**

Tribox (Japan): **tribox.cart.fc2.com**

V-CUBES (Greece): **www.v-cubes.com**

A nice selection of very special, high-quality, handmade rotational puzzles can be found at: (Scott) Bedard Puzzles: **www.bedardpuzzles.com**. General information on all kinds of rotational puzzles, including the newest designs, can be found at **www.twistypuzzles.com/forum**. Solutions for all kinds of rotational puzzles are presented by Jaap Scherphuis at his Web site: **www.geocities.com/jaapsch/puzzles**.

NEW ROTATIONAL PUZZLES

Pyraminx and Skewb

Uwe Meffert, born in Wernigerode, Germany, on November 28, 1939, invented a puzzle called the Pyraminx several years before the Rubik's Cube™ went on sale. In the early 1970s, while he was doing research into whether handling different solid shapes such as pyramids and cubes had any influence on one's well-being and bio-energy flow, Meffert discovered that holding polygon shapes like the tetrahedron and dodecahedron had a gentle massaging and stimulating influence and instilled a sense of peace, relaxation, and calm. He was encouraged to change the pyramid/tetrahedron shape into a game or puzzle. His initial concept of a tetrahedron-shaped object was improved by Meffert and his brother, a brilliant engineer, with a simple mechanism that allowed the parts of the pyramid to move relative to each other. The initial sample, named the Pyraminx, was made from varnished wood.

It was years later when, due to the worldwide excitement generated by the Rubik's Cube™, he was encouraged to try to market the Pyraminx as a puzzle. He traveled to Hong Kong and Japan and found several companies

UWE MEFFERT

PYRAMINX

TETRAMINX

interested in making and selling his puzzle. The Pyraminx was received with enthusiasm everywhere it was sold, and the demand for it suddenly became overwhelming. Soon the puzzle was being made in huge quantities in Hong Kong and Japan by such toy producers as Qualidux, Tomy, Tsukuda, and Bandi. Meffert, who was granted a patent in 1981, claims that 90 million Pyraminx puzzles were sold within three years. The Pyraminx has 933,120 possible positions and can be solved in eleven moves (ignoring the ornamental tips). Taiwanese and Russian versions of Meffert's Tetraminx have been produced. In 1982, Meffert published a catalog containing fourteen new rotational puzzles. Most of these, however, were never put into production.

Tony Durham invented another puzzle, the Skewb, which was produced by Meffert and initially called Pyraminx Cube. However, Douglas Hofstadter introduced the name Skewb in an article in *Scientific American* in 1982, and it has been used ever since. Both the Pyraminx and the Skewb puzzles are based on four rotational axes. However, their internal mechanisms are different. The Pyraminx is built around a sphere and the Skewb is built around a four-armed spider. The six squares of the Skewb correspond to the six edge pieces of the Pyraminx.

The mechanism of the Skewb can be rather confusing at first. It is also remarkable in the sense that pieces of all six sides of the puzzle move simultaneously when the puzzle is rotated. The Skewb has 3,149,280 possible positions and can be solved in eleven moves.

SKEWB

SKEWB DIAMOND

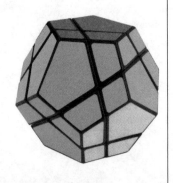

SKEWB ULTIMATE

GOLDEN EGG

MICKEY SKEWB BALL

MACH MAGIC BALL

MEGAMINX PUZZLE

Some new puzzles based on the Skewb mechanism are the Skewb Ultimate, Skewb Diamond, Mickey Skewb Ball, and Golden Egg, which were all produced by Meffert. Gyula Mach, a Hungarian company, produced the Mach Magic Ball.

Megaminx Puzzle and Variations

The Megaminx puzzle was invented almost simultaneously by several people, and it appeared on the market soon after the Rubik's Cube™. It has a dodecahedron shape with twelve faces that can be rotated and twenty corners. The dodecahedron may appear to be much more difficult than the 3×3×3; however, the corners of the puzzles are very much alike and the difficulty in solving them is about the same. Hence, it is not surprising that after the introduction of the Rubik's Cube™, several inventors and patents for this dodecahedron puzzle emerged, and several of the designs have been produced. The most common one is the Megaminx by Uwe Meffert, who bought the patent rights from Kersten Meier and Ben Halpern. Other inventors of these puzzles are Christoph Bandelow, Helmut Corbeck, and Szlivka Ferenc. Ferenc's patent is related to the Hungarian Supernova. Another version is produced by the Japanese toy company Tomy, and there is also a version produced in China and three versions in Malaysia. Some versions use six colors and have 6.1×10^{63} possible positions, and others have twelve colors with 1×10^{68} possible positions.

A derivative of the Megaminx proposed by Meffert in his 1982 catalogue is called the Pyraminx Crystal. Recently, two independent inventers—Katsuhiko Okamoto and Aleh Hladzilin—produced versions of this puzzle, called Mega Crystal and Aleh's Brilic, respectively. As a result of the success of these handcrafted models, Uwe Meffert decided in 2008 to produce this puzzle.

Adam Alexander created a puzzle called Alexander's Star in the shape of a great dodecahedron, and he was granted a patent in 1985. Two versions of Alexander's Star were marketed, one with stickers and one with painted colors. The initial design of Alexander's Star uses six colors for twelve stars, resulting in 7.2×10^{34} possible positions. The puzzle is very difficult to solve, however, and the stars do not turn smoothly.

PYRAMINX CRYSTAL

ALEXANDER'S STAR

The dual version of the dodecahedron, in terms of platonic solids, is the icosahedron, which has twenty faces and twelve corners. The Dogic puzzle, which has twenty axes, was patented by Hungarians Zoltan and Robert Vecsei in 1998 and marketed by their company Vecsö. It had twelve different colors, one for each corner, and 2.2×10^{82} possible positions. Unfortunately, only relatively few samples were made before the production tool broke. Partly as a result of this problem, and partly due to the uniqueness of the puzzle, it became extremely rare and expensive. After production stopped, its price on eBay exceeded $500 for each puzzle. To take advantage of the demand for these puzzles, Meffert acquired the molds in 2004 and started a new production in 2005. Meffert also introduced versions with two, five, and ten colors.

The Impossiball

This Impossiball or Incrediball, invented by William Gustafson in 1984, has twelve axes just like the Megaminx, but it has a spherical shape. It was produced in the early 1980s by Milton Bradley. The Impossiball is a rounded icosahedron puzzle. To allow the movements of the pieces, the twenty triangular shaped parts fit into an array of twelve soft-rubber axes. This makes the alignment of the pieces of the puzzle a bit flexible. Turning parts of the puzzle is not easy. Several years after the introduction, a new production run was made by Meffert with the puzzles having either six or twelve colors. The Impossiball has a nice feature of being able to easily remove a single triangular part. In this way, a type of sliding piece puzzle is created on a spherical surface.

The Thomas Ball also has twelve axes of rotation with each axis attached to a fixed black pentagonal piece that is surrounded by five movable hexagonal pieces. These pieces slide underneath the black caps at the ends of the rotation axes. Thomas Balls were invented and patented by Zdenek Blazek and Miroslav Jandora in 2003 and marketed by Brainy Toys of the Czech Republic. Initially six main types were introduced, with various artwork.

DOGIC PUZZLE

For the twelve color Impossiball and the Thomas Ball, the number of possible positions is 2.4×10^{25}.

Masterball

The Masterball, which was invented and patented by Hungarian engineer and lawyer Geza Gyovai in 1989, is another rotational puzzle that was produced in large quantities. The puzzle consists of four layers, which are divided in eight equal sections.

Instead of stickers, artwork is printed on the puzzles. At the official Masterball Web site, six different types are mentioned, but several other variations have also been produced. When all of the sections are different colors or designs, the Masterball has 2.7×10^{25} possible positions.

A related version of the Masterball is the Logi-Vip Ball, which was made by Arxon. The Logi-Vip Ball also has four layers and eight sections but it can only be rotated around one cutting plane at a time. Each of the eight sections has four layers with graded shades of the same basic color, making each piece different and creating a very attractive puzzle. It was invented by Hubert Petutschnig and patented in 1981.

Square-1

When Vojtech Kopsky and Karel Hrsel were working on the concept of the Square-1 puzzle, they considered many different shapes and finally they came up with the concept of "Back to Square-1," for which they received a patent in 1993. The Square-1 puzzle changes into confusing shapes as you twist it. The puzzle must be restored to a cube shape before the colors can be solved. The puzzle consists of eighteen pieces with eight having a center vertex of 30 degrees and eight having a 60 degree vertex. The middle layer consists of two pieces that are connected by a screw around which the entire puzzle can be rotated as two halves. Several manufacturers have produced and marketed the puzzle using different names, such as Cube21 and Super Cubix.

Another version of the same puzzle concept that is actually older than the Square-1 puzzle itself is the Olidjus puzzle. It contains eighteen sections in the top and bottom layers and has only two sections in the middle layer. These two sections are disguised by nine divisions per section. Hence, the cutting plane of the puzzle must be determined from the small circles at

PUCK PUZZLE

BRAINBALL

GERDIG UFO

either end of the puzzle. The puzzle was designed and made in Russia by Dimitriew, Jurin, and Stulnikow.

Puck, Rubik's UFO, and Related Puzzles

Another puzzle with rotation around a fixed axis is the Puck puzzle. Geza Csomos, Udulo Mszmp, and Zoltan Pataki patented it in 1991. The puzzle consists of a disk with twelve equal-sized pieces in an outer circle and two halves in an inner circle. By rotating the inner circle, it is possible to change the cutting plane. A large number of variations with different imprinted designs have been produced. Another similar puzzle with six pieces in the outer circle is known as Kep Korong. The printed designs on the sides of the puzzle have included a cat, a dog, and E.T.

The Puck puzzles resemble another disk-like puzzle called Rubik's Cheese. This puzzle is relatively rare and was produced in Hungary. Despite the two-layer coloring, the Rubik's Cheese has only a single layer, consisting of six pieces that can rotate randomly. The puzzle is easy to solve. Other similar puzzles are the BrainBall by Andreas Unsicker, the Gerdig UFO by

Gerhard Huncaga, Smart Alex by Dumitru Pop, the Sando Ring, and the Octo Ring.

Dino Cubes

The Dino Cube is a puzzle that is based on eight axes of rotation and turns in a rather peculiar way. At each corner, three different pieces meet, which can rotate together around the corner in steps of 120

DINO CUBES

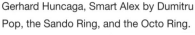

degrees. Since the puzzle consists of only twelve pieces and since only three pieces are turned simultaneously, the puzzle is relatively easy to solve. Unlike the Rubik's Cube™, pieces of the Dino Cube are oriented correctly automatically when they are in the correct place. The first samples of the Dino Cube were designed and made

out of paper independently by Robert Webb from Australia and Stephen Harvey from New Zealand. Mass production of the Dino Cube began in 1995 by S.Y. Liou, who also invented the original Dino Cube.

There are a couple of other puzzles that are based on an eight-axis movement similar to the puzzles mentioned above, but which have a different look.

The first of these is a puzzle that we'll call the Dino Star. This puzzle has the shape of a stella octangula, and movement is possible by turning one of each of the eight tips. This results in the movement of three pieces that are positioned in a circle that surrounds the tetrahedron tips. The second puzzle, BrainTwist, has essentially the same solution. It was patented by Charles Hoberman and Matthew Davis on May 12, 2005. Last, there is the Tripod, Jackpot, or Platypus puzzle, which was invented by Yusuf Seyhan and made in several variations.

The Rainbow Cube, can be considered a truncated Dino Cube. Two versions were made in Japan with either seven or fourteen colors.

The Void Cube

Ernő Rubik astonished the world with his cube puzzle and its amazing internal mechanism. It consists of a central six-armed spider cross core and two types of pieces (eight corner pieces and twelve edge pieces) that are designed so the pieces support each other.

It is equally astonishing that Katsuhiko Okamoto has succeeded in creating a 3×3×3 rotating cube puzzle without the spider core! His invention is called Void Cube. Instead of Rubik's spider core, he uses twenty moving pieces with six hollow axes. It applies a special kind of tiny rail to allow the movement of the pieces. The Void Cube won the Jury Grand Prize at the 2007 International Puzzle Party in Australia. Production of the puzzle in Japan began in 2008.

Handcrafted Rotational Puzzles

At least fifty designers have created hundreds of different handmade variations of puzzles, including brand-new designs of rotational puzzles. Only a small fraction of all of these handcrafted puzzles are described here, including a few of the leading creators in this growing field.

In December 1981, close to the peak of the Cube craze, *Tony Fisher* modified two Rubik's Cubes™ and joined them along one edge to make his "Siamese Cubes," probably the first handmade, modified rotational puzzle. Fisher, who lives in England, became the pioneer in the design and crafting of new handcrafted puzzles because he "got fed up waiting for new puzzles to come out." Since 1981, Fisher has designed and crafted about 100 puzzles based on different puzzle mechanisms.

Puzzle modification requires insight, as well as skills in puzzle design and manufacturing. Puzzles having a different numbers of layers along at least two

axes—cuboids in particular—require some rather complicated tricks in order to be functional. One trick involves the technique of shifting cutting planes. It was invented in 1995 by Fisher for his 3×3×4 cuboid puzzle and subsequently applied to his 2×3×4, 3×3×5, and 4×4×5 puzzles. Another technique, initially developed by Geert Hellings, rounded the center pieces of a regular 4×4×4 cube to create additional turning layers for a uniform 2×2×4 and a nonuniform 2×2×6. This technique was further perfected by Fisher to create fully functional and uniform 2×2×6, 2×2×7, and 4×4×6 cuboids.

One of Fisher's most beautiful puzzle modifications—and one that most people consider his best puzzle—was originally intended to be called the Millennium Cube. However, designing and making it took a bit longer than expected, and it wasn't ready in time for the millennium. When the puzzle was finally finished, he named it the Golden Cube. Made from a Skewb, the Golden Cube is surprisingly difficult to solve. This remarkable puzzle is the first rotational puzzle that has just one color and requires the solver to restore the cube shape. Moreover, the beautiful appearance

3×3×5 CUBOID

2×2×6 CUBOID

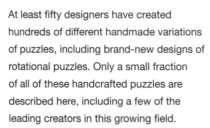

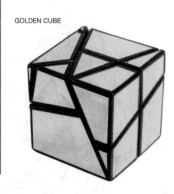

GOLDEN CUBE

GOLDEN CUBE SCRAMBLED

OVERLAPPING CUBE

of the puzzle, including its single-color design, makes the Golden Cube one of the most intriguing puzzles ever made.

Another Fisher innovation is the Overlapping Cube. For this modification, Fisher made optimum use of the mechanism of the 4×4×4 cube manufactured by Eastsheen. Fisher extended some of its hidden internal parts to make the puzzle more difficult. Hollow edge pieces allow the passage of neighboring pieces, making the puzzle 'overlapping'.

Finally, his Hexaminx puzzle, a cubic version of the Megaminx puzzle, was created in 2007. It is a complex transformation and involved developing new manufacturing techniques, including production of new parts cast with polyurethane resin. Fisher believes these techniques are a "stepping stone to new and possibly more complex puzzles."

Jean Claude Constantin is a professional designer and maker of all types of mechanical puzzles, and he established his own successful puzzle business in Germany more than 20 years ago. He started creating rotational puzzle transformations in 1988, and by 1995, he had designed about 100 new puzzles. His favorite, and the best selling among all of his designs, is the Mushroom Puzzle. Constantin is fascinated to see how existing puzzles can be transformed into other shapes. He combined parts of different puzzles and made puzzle extensions, typically using wood. He has created puzzles in shapes that appeal to children and adults alike.

MUSHROOM

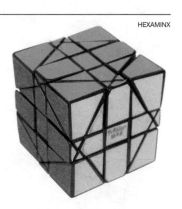

HEXAMINX

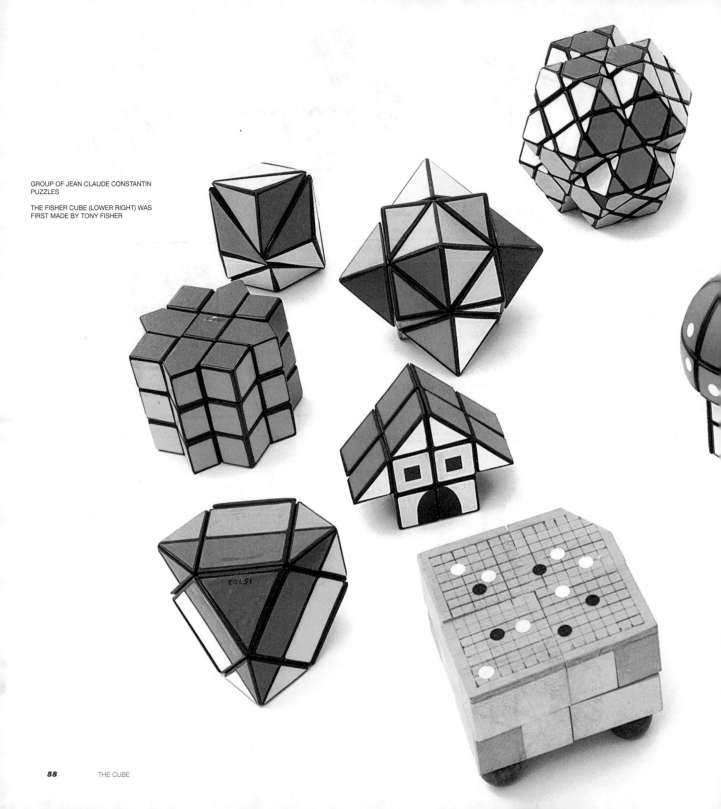

GROUP OF JEAN CLAUDE CONSTANTIN
PUZZLES

THE FISHER CUBE (LOWER RIGHT) WAS
FIRST MADE BY TONY FISHER

MASTER OCTAHEDRON

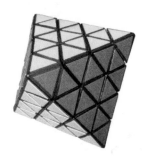

BRILICUBE

CURVED MASTERMORPHIX

Aleh Hladzilin is another early designer and craftsman of rotational puzzles. He made his first puzzle—a fully functional 3×3×5 cuboid—in 1989, before he moved from Belarus to the United States. Of the thirteen puzzles he has created, he is especially proud of his amazing Master Octahedron, Brilicube, and Curved Mastermorphix. His Brilicube looks like a Square-1 puzzle on all six faces. It is a 3×3×3 cube with the six center pieces hidden. The cutting planes appear to be impossible to rotate, but function because of the use of hollow pieces. Hladzilin probably was the first to truncate a 3×3×3 cube into a curved, pillowed tetrahedron shape, which he named Curved Mastermorphix. He also made an early version of the Pyraminx Crystal, which is now in production.

Katsuhiko Okamoto began designing and crafting new rotational puzzles in Japan in 2001. His first puzzle was a 2×2×3 cuboid he named Slimtower. Since then, he has created thirty-one rotational puzzles. He states that his goal is to achieve "the design that seems at first to be impossible." He has attained this goal on multiple occasions, particularly with his Void Cube, Bevel Cube, and Floppy Cube. His seemingly impossible Void Cube is hollow with no center pieces. It is now in production in Japan and is discussed on page 55. The Bevel Cube appears to have cutting planes of a 2×2×2 cube, but the triangular sections at the corners rotate. Okamoto had to create a new mechanism for it to work. The puzzle is identical to the independently developed Helicopter Cube, which is discussed later. His incredible Floppy Cube, a 1×3×3 cuboid, also appears to be impossible to rotate, but it is fully functional. He also created a version of the Pyraminx Crystal, now in production, and he made a version of the Pyracue that was first designed by Ishino.

PYRACUE

VOID CUBE

FLOPPY CUBE

BEVEL CUBE

STAIR CUBE

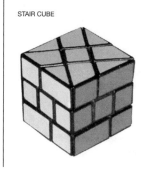

BUMP CUBE

TRICK DOMINOES

Another well-known Japanese puzzle inventor and maker is **_Hidetoshi Takeji_**. His first design was the Stair Cube, which he crafted from a 3×3×3 cube four years ago. Since then, he has created eleven more original rotational puzzles. He is best known for his Bump Cube, which is now commercially available as the Mirror Cube. The puzzle is made from a 3×3×3 cube with pieces of unequal size. This results in all kinds of peculiar shapes when the puzzle is rotated. He says that one of the reasons that he likes the puzzle is "when it is scrambled, the shape looks like a Manhattan Skyscraper." His Trick Dominoes, made from 2×3×3 mechanisms, are really a pair of puzzles, which look identical from above but are mirror images when looking from below. The two puzzles have different rotational movements.

Hidetoshi has a wonderful sense of humor. When asked what he enjoys most about designing and making his puzzles, he said: "Usually I imagine a scene with a dandy sitting in a chair playing with my puzzles in front of the fireplace. He sips his drink of brandy, while listening to classical music, and rotates the puzzle in an expansive mood." He adds, "I live in Japan, and there are no fireplaces."

British puzzle creator **_Anthony Greenhill_** says he "sort of drifted into making puzzles" in 2002. His problem was that he caught the serious collecting bug too late, when it was not possible to buy many of the early production cube puzzles with modified shapes, such as the Cuboctahedron or the Rhombic Dodecahedron. So he decided to make them himself for his collection. Soon he became more adventurous and began making dodecahedrons, icosahedrons, and tetrahedrons from Cubes and Skewbs. He likes to figure out how to take a production puzzle, such as a Square-1 Cube, and transform it into a dodecahedron. In fact, that was his first original design, which he called Greenhill's Dodecahedron.

The design of his next original puzzle, Greenhill's 5 Layer Square-1, was challenging. After a couple of false starts and blind alleys, he succeeded in creating the puzzle from the Square-1 core mechanism. Greenhill's Tetrahedron also used the Square-1 mechanism and was a difficult design with a complex inner core. Scrambling the puzzle leads to amazing shapes, which challenge some solvers to ask, "Where do I start?"

GREENHILL'S DODECAHEDRON

GREENHILL'S 5 LAYER SQUARE-1

GREENHILL'S CUBE

GREENHILL'S 1

GREENHILL'S TETRAHEDRON

American **_Lee Tutt_** entered the world of original puzzle designers in 2005 by creating a truncated icosahedron Buckyball-shaped puzzle called Tuttminx. He designed the puzzle on his computer and discovered that stereo lithography techniques used in the manufacture of fine jewelry could be used to make masters of the pieces of the puzzle. Tutt designed and handcrafted a 32-axis spider core for this puzzle, which consists of 182 external pieces. Since then, he has designed seven original rotational puzzles and modified four other designs. One of his best original designs is the Pentagonal Prism, which was shown as a cardboard concept model in Meffert's 1982 catalog, but it had never been made.

Tutt considers the Icosaminx his prettiest design. He used a concept of the puzzle by Ryan Thompson and extended the shape to an icosahedron with functional tips. His most complex puzzle design, and the puzzle that he is rightfully the most proud of, is his impossible-looking Holey Megaminx. He was inspired by Katsuhiko Okamoto's Void Cube to design a version of the Megaminx puzzle that, like the Void Cube, has hollow axes. The Holey Megaminx essentially consists of just three master parts that snap together when assembled. It is very difficult to make adjustments, so the parts have to be extremely accurate. This spectacular puzzle is the prime example of Tutt's creativity in puzzle design, as well as his extraordinary craftsmanship.

Anthony challenged himself to create an original cube puzzle. Greenhill's Cube was created from a Diamond 3×3×3 Cube stood on a corner, and then a cube was built around it. To create Greenhill's 1, he "went back to Square-1" for the core mechanism. It is his favorite original rotational puzzle because, "on initial sight, it is not obvious how it works, and it just looks quiet and simple in appearance."

TUTTMINX

HOLEY MEGAMINX

PENTAGONAL PRISM

TUTT'S ICOSAMINX

MEFFERT CATALOG PENTAGON

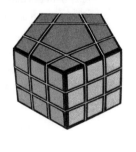

HELICOPTER CUBE

SUPERX

3×3×5 CUBOID

3×3×3 EGG

Adam Cowan, another American, started working on his first original design of a rotational puzzle in 2005. That design would become his Helicopter Cube. It turned out to be more interesting than he expected because of its ability to be scrambled not only with 180-degree turns but also with partial turns. This "jumbleable" property adds an additional level of difficulty to the puzzle. Another of his designs, the SuperX, was inspired by a design that he found in a patent. It amazingly combines the movements of a 2×2×2 cube and a Dino cube in one puzzle. He considered his Cubic 3×3×5 cuboid just a "curiosity" when he modeled the parts in just an hour, but when he played with it he found it much more interesting than he expected. His 3×3×3 Egg is a shape transformation of a 3×3×3 cube oriented on the long diagonal corner-to-corner axis of the cube. He says, "It is a very interesting puzzle that is solved by the shape, and its smooth, curved surface makes it fit nicely into your hand." Inspired by Fisher's Golden Cube, Cowan recently created a new design with his goal "to make a 3×3×3 cube as confusing and difficult as possible, with only one solution." The result is the Ghost Cube,

which has the mechanism at an odd angle and the layers misaligned with each other, and the puzzle is solved by shape, not color. When asked what he enjoys the most about designing and crafting rotational puzzles, Adam wrote, "The best moment is when I hold one of my designs in my hand for the first time. I get to see and touch a puzzle that was at one time only an idea."

GHOST CUBE, SOLVED

GHOST CUBE, SCRAMBLED

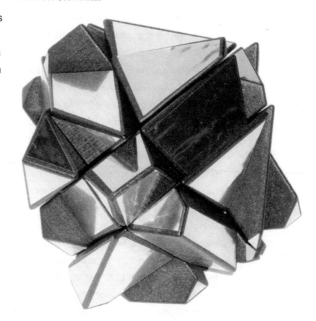

Matt Shepit, who lives in New Zealand, began designing puzzles in 2006. His first design was the transformation of a UFO puzzle into a dodecahedron. However, he found out he was not the first to design and make this puzzle. Since then, he has designed over fifty rotational puzzles. He has fabricated thirteen of them and is working to complete three more. He is the most proud of his 24-Cube, also known as "Little Chop." Unlike the Dino cube, the 24 Cube puzzle rotates along any of the six cutting planes that divide the puzzle into two halves. The puzzle concept, he says, is "fairly obvious," and many people had proposed and worked on the puzzle since the mid-1980s, but he was the first to design a mechanism that would work and then craft a fully functional model. The complexity of the puzzle is illustrated by the fact that 209 pieces are required for the puzzle, but it has only twenty-four visible outside pieces. His other original designs include Rua, the Danger Cube, and the Cheeseblock. Rua means "two" in the Te Reo Maori language, and Shepit chose that name because each face has a 2×2 look to it. The puzzle is a face-turning rhombic dodecahedron. The Danger Cube got its name because of an accident that occurred while crafting the puzzle. It is based on the Square-1 puzzle, but its shape is an elegant-looking pillowed tetrahedron. The name Cheeseblock was used because of the puzzle's similarity to Rubik's Cheese, but in block form. The concept is simple, but it turned out to be quite complicated to combine Square-1 mechanisms with the 2×2×2 cube. Shepit is very pleased with the result, and it is the best-received puzzle he has designed.

CHEESEBLOCK

MASTER TETRAHEDRON

GIGAMINX

TERAMINX

Considering that ***Andrew Cormier*** only began designing original rotational puzzles in January 2008, his accomplishments are truly remarkable. He has already designed and built six original puzzles. He was still experimenting with different printing and casting methods when he built his first two puzzles—the Master Tetrahedron and Elite Tetrahedron—and they turned out too loose and not satisfactory. He later redesigned these puzzles, and his new designs work very well. The puzzles are not loose, and never jam. One of his favorite puzzles is the Gigaminx v1.5, a two-layered version of the Megaminx. The first fully functional Gigaminx was designed and made by Tyler Fox and, since it was demonstrated, several improved versions have been designed and fabricated by Fox and others.

Cormier's favorite design is the Teraminx, an amazing three-layered version of the Megaminx puzzle. He wrote when he finished it, "This puzzle puts a smile on my face." It is no wonder, since the puzzle consists of 542 outer pieces and has 1.2×10^{573} different possible positions.

The Teraminx is the most complicated handcrafted puzzle described in this section, and the logical closure of the hundreds of handcrafted puzzle modifications and new puzzles that have been made by dozens of inventors.

The puzzle designers and their puzzles described above represent only a small fraction of the handcrafted puzzle trend. Techniques such as CAD and 3-D printing (rapid prototyping) have had a major positive influence on the introduction of new and often very complicated designs. Although many puzzle designers and makers will still be involved in mechanically constructing and improving their puzzles, computer tools now available make completely new designs possible.

Many modifications of puzzles were made in the 1980s, but activity dropped off in the '90s. During the last four years, however, there has been a large increase in the number of people involved in making new rotational puzzles and puzzle modifications. One of the major factors in this resurgence is the puzzle forum on the Web site **twistypuzzles.com/ forum**, which was initiated by Wayne Johnson and provides easy instant communication between designers. The sharing of information about the latest designs and completed puzzles from all over the world stimulates others to try to improve on what has been done.

Chapter 4

Solutions to All the Cube Puzzles

By Wei-Hwa Huang
and Dieter Gebhardt

 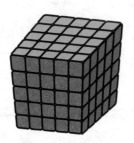 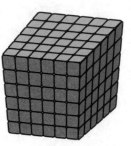 

Introduction

The solutions for all the rotational cube puzzles in production today are provided in this chapter. We begin with the most common puzzle, the 3×3×3, and then cover those of other sizes, from the 2×2×2 up to the 7×7×7.

The solution for the 3×3×3 is thoroughly explained with accompanying illustrations provided as necessary.* We have designed the solution instructions to enable a beginner who has never solved a cube puzzle before (perhaps you) to do so successfully. In addition, the solutions will provide an important foundation as well as an introduction to the terms, notation, and move sequences that will be built upon in the larger and more complex cube puzzles.

As you solve the 3×3×3 cube, you will learn sequences of moves that are useful for all cubes. These sequences will be shown in detail for the 3×3×3, but with fewer diagrams and more referral to the previous work as we progress to the larger

cubes. Unlike many other solutions on the market today, our solutions generalize easily to cubes of all sizes, and the same basic sequences will be useful for all of them. Each cube is made up of small indivisible cubes called **cubies**. (Technically a cubie is not really a cube, but a piece of plastic that appears to be a cube on the outside surface.) As the puzzle gets larger, the number of cubies increases. The table at the top of the next page shows how many cubies on each cube are movable and, therefore, must be placed and oriented properly to solve each of the cube puzzles.

> **✳** Small bits of information that may be of interest to those who want to know more about cube solving will appear in special asterisked boxes like this one. They will never be necessary to the solution but may help you understand things better.

Cube Sizes	Movable Cubies
2×2×2	8
3×3×3	20
4×4×4	56
5×5×5	92
6×6×6	152
7×7×7	212

✱ For the cubes with an odd number of cubies on an edge, the number at left doesn't include the six face center cubies, as some experimentation will show you that they can never move (relative to each other). However, if your cube has pictures on the faces, the orientation of these face cubies can matter. We'll show you how to deal with that in a later sidebar.

Terminology

The following terms are very important for understanding and solving cube puzzles. They are used throughout our solutions (and by many English-speaking cube solvers around the world), so it is important that you become familiar with them before attempting to follow our instructions.

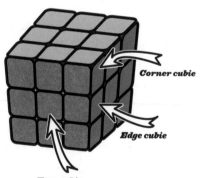

Corner cubie

Edge cubie

Face cubie
THE THREE BASIC TYPES OF CUBIES

The Cube: The puzzle. The Cube is composed of **layers** that can be turned. Each layer is made up of **cubies**. The Cube can be 2×2×2, 3×3×3, 4×4×4, or bigger.

Cubie: The smallest external part of the Cube. A cubie can have three stickers (**corner cubie**), two stickers (**edge cubie**), or one sticker (**face cubie**) of various colors attached to it. The 3×3×3, for example, has 26 cubies (eight corners, twelve edges, and six faces).

Face: One of six sides of the Cube. We call the six faces of the Cube Up (U), Down (D), Front (F), Back (B), Left (L), and Right (R). When the Cube is solved, all of the sides of the cubies that show on each face are the same color (or part of a picture).

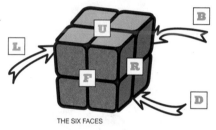

THE SIX FACES

"B" stands for "Back," not "Bottom." When you see the letter B used, be careful!

(Messages accompanied with a question mark, like this one, explain common points of confusion or clarify things that trip up many people. Best to read these, especially if you're confused.)

The cubies being defined are depicted in yellow in the diagrams on this page.

Face cubie: A cubie that is on the face of the cube. It has only one color. The 3×3×3 only has one face cubie on each face, and they are also center cubies.

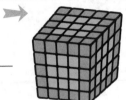

5x5x5 FACE CUBIES

5×5×5 CENTERS

Center cubie: A face cubie that is at the center of the face. They only exist on odd-sized Cubes. Since the center cubies never move relative to each other, they can always be used to determine the correct color arrangement even when the rest of the cube is messed up.

Corner cubie: A cubie that is on a corner of the Cube. It has three differently colored stickers. All of the Cube puzzles have eight corner cubies.

3x3x3 CORNERS

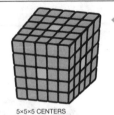

4×4×4 CENTERS

Edge cubie: A cubie that is on an edge of the cube. It has two differently colored stickers. The 3×3×3 Cube has twelve edge cubies, the 2×2×2 has none, and the larger cubes have more.

Middle edge cubie: An edge cubie that is on the mid-point of the edge. On the 3×3×3 Cube, all edge cubies are middle edge cubies, so we don't bother using this term.

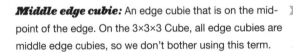

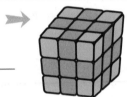

5x5x5 MIDDLE EDGES

5×5×5 SIDE EDGES

Side edge cubie: An edge cubie that is not a middle edge cubie. On even-sized cubes such as the 4×4×4 Cube, all edge cubies are side edge cubies.

Naming Cubies vs. Naming Positions: A position is a location for a cubie, usually designated by the faces the cubie is on. Usually this is based on the parts of the cube that are already solved. For example, the "UF position" (or "UF edge") is the location of the edge cubie that is on the Up and Front face. The "UF cubie," on the other hand, refers to the cubie that should belong in the UF position when the cube is solved—even if the cubie is currently at a different location!

THE *UF* EDGE CUBIE IS IN THE *FR* POSITION

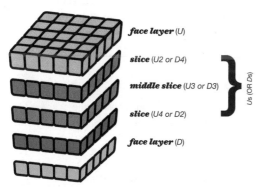

face layer (U)

slice (U2 or D4)

middle slice (U3 or D3)

slice (U4 or D2)

face layer (D)

Us (OR Ds)

THE *U* AND *D* (AND RELATED) LAYERS ON THE 5×5×5

Move: Rotating a single layer (or, for the larger cubes, a group of connected layers). Occasionally we'll use the word in its generic sense (e.g., "Our next goal is to move the DR edge to the UF position").

Turn: Some solvers use this as a special term, to mean a move that is a simple 90-degree rotation between two layers (hence, a 90-degree **slice** move is two "turns," and a 180-degree rotation is two "turns"). We don't use this as a special term, but we'll sometimes use it for moves ("turn the U layer clockwise") and we'll occasionally use it to refer to reorienting the entire cube (e.g., "turn the cube upside-down so that the UFR corner is now the DFL corner").

Some books are very precise with the order of letters when naming their positions and cubies, mainly because of twists and flips (see next page); for example, "UFR position" and "FRU position" are the same position but with a different cubie orientation. We won't bother with this distinction.

Layer: The smallest group of cubies that can be moved together. The layers on the end (that contain an entire face) are often named after the corresponding face (e.g., "The U layer"), and the other layers are called **slices**.

Slice: A layer that is not a face (see above). Odd-sized cubies will have a **middle slice**. We tend to number our slices based on a parallel face layer (e.g., "U2"), and use a lowercase "s" to refer to all the slices parallel to that direction when moved as a group (e.g., "Fs").

A 90-DEGREE SLICE MOVE CAN BE CONSIDERED TWO "TURNS" BY SOME

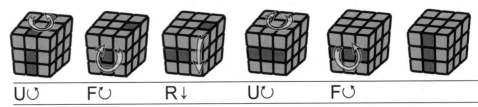

U↺   F↻   R↓   U↺   F↻

SEQUENCE K₁ FROM SECTION 3.6, FOUND LATER IN THIS BOOK*

In case you're curious, the main purpose of Sequence K₁ is to flip the UF edge while leaving the rest of the Rs slice undisturbed.

Sequence: A series of moves that changes the cube in a predictable way. Most methods of solving the cube involve looking for the positions of certain cubies on the cube, then executing sequences to move them into the correct position (and/or orientation). Sequences often focus on changing one section of the cube while ignoring other sections of the cube (which the sequence might mess up); when we depict a sequence, we'll portray the sections to be ignored in gray, as in the diagram above.

THE UFR CUBIE IS POSITIONED CORRECTLY BUT NOT ORIENTED CORRECTLY

Positioned Correctly: When a cubie is in the correct position. For example, if the UFR corner cubie (the cubie with the U, F, and R colors on it) is in the UFR position (the corner cubie position common to the U, F, and R layers), then it is positioned correctly. A cubie that is positioned correctly may not yet be **oriented correctly**, though.

THE UFR CUBIE IS ORIENTED CORRECTLY BUT NOT POSITIONED CORRECTLY

Oriented Correctly: When a cubie has been spun or flipped such that its colors match the face colors. (Usually this term only applies to cubies that are positioned correctly, as it is a bit ambiguous otherwise, but it might occasionaly be used to refer to one face-color matching, as in the diagram at left.) The Cube is solved when all cubies are positioned correctly and oriented correctly.

Twist: To reorient a corner cubie such that it is in the same position but has its colors pointing in different directions.

THREE DIFFERENT WAYS TO TWIST THE UFR CUBIE

Flip: To reorient a *center* edge cubie such that it is in the same position but has its colors swapped.

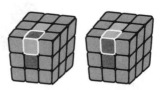

TWO WAYS TO FLIP THE FR CUBIE

It seems like they can, but side edge cubies *cannot* be flipped. (We'll tell you why in section 4.3.)

Solving the 3×3×3 Cube

If you're just joining us, you'll probably want to read the "Terminology" section on the last few pages to make sure we're, well, on the same page.

Here's our general approach.*

3.1
Solve Corners in One Layer

"A" SEQUENCES

3.2
Solve Edges in the Same Layer

"E" SEQUENCES

3.3
Solve the Remaining Corners

"C" AND "A" SEQUENCES

3.4
Solve the Opposite Layer Edges

"G" SEQUENCES

3.5
Position the Remaining Edges

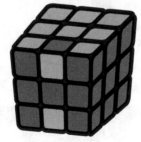

"H" SEQUENCES

3.6
Orient the Remaining Edges

"K" SEQUENCES

* Our method is great for learning and easy to memorize, but it's not so great if you want to break speed records. Speed-cubing systems require a lot of memorization and are optimized for few moves on few faces, which has the advantage that fewer moves are needed. However, it's harder to see why their sequences work. We hope that our method will help you understand more *why* than *how*, and so help you remember how to solve the cube for years to come. If you're interested in moving into the realm of speedcubing, by all means check out the many web sites on the other methods (after you read ours, of course).

3.0
Getting to Know the Cube

Most solvers tend to hold the cube in the left hand while turning faces with the right hand*; accordingly, we'll mostly be having you turn the Up (U), Front (F), and Right (R) layers. Our standard diagram (depicted to the right) therefore is optimized for displaying the U, F, and R faces.

Since actual cubes come in a wide variety of colors, with different manufacturers using different color arrangements, we don't want to confuse you with an arrangement that is close to your cube but arranged differently. So, we'll be using some nonstandard colors for the six faces, as well as using gray for faces we don't particularly care about at the moment.

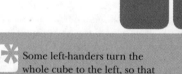

CYAN	PURPLE	BROWN	LIME	PINK	TAN	GRAY

Some left-handers turn the whole cube to the left, so that the "Front" face is facing left and the "Right" face is facing toward them.

Occasionally we'll need to refer to the other three faces of the cubes—Down (D), Left (L), and Back (B). When depicting them, we'll use the "flap" notation as seen to the left; imagine the hidden faces as if the cube were a partially unfolded box.

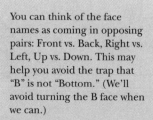

You can think of the face names as coming in opposing pairs: Front vs. Back, Right vs. Left, Up vs. Down. This may help you avoid the trap that "B" is not "Bottom." (We'll avoid turning the B face when we can.)

Notation* for moving U and D.

Most experts use a different notation for turns (invented by David Singmaster, a contributor to this book), where U means clockwise, U' (or U⁻¹) means counterclockwise, and U² means 180°. We use our notation because you won't need to tilt your cube around to figure out which way is clockwise and we can avoid ambiguity with slice moves, but be aware of this difference when reading about the Cube elsewhere. Singmaster versions of the moves will be supplied on the summary page.

You might ask, why don't we use the same sort of arrows for U as we do for D? Because a lot of people think of "turn to the right" as clockwise, so for us to use U→ to mean counterclockwise would be really confusing. So U, and only U, gets special treatment.

U↺: Turn the Up layer counterclockwise 90°.

U↻: Turn the Up layer clockwise 90°.

U↻↻: Turn the Up layer 180°. (This is the same as U↺↺.) Note the yellow double-arrowhead.

D→: Turn the Down* layer to the right 90° (clockwise if you are looking from below).

D←: Turn the Down layer to the left 90° (counterclockwise).

D→→: Turn the Down layer face 180°. (This is the same as D←←.)

R↑: Turn the Right face upward (clockwise) 90°.

R↓ and R↑↑ (not shown): follow similarly.

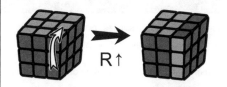

R↑

Moving the R and F faces.

FↃ: Turn the Front face clockwise 90°.

FↃ and FↃↃ (not shown): follow similarly.

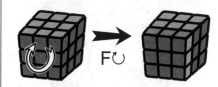

FↃ

Us→: Move the second layer from the top to the right 90°. This is the same as Ds→, as the second layer from the top is the same as the second layer from the bottom. This in-between layer is called a "slice."

Us← and Us→→ (not shown): follow similarly.

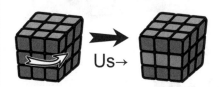

Us→

Rs↑: Turn the slice between the R and L layers upward 90°.

Rs↓ and Rs↑↑ (not shown): follow similarly.

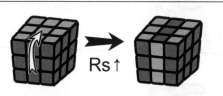

Rs↑

FsↃ: Turn the slice between the F and B layers clockwise 90°.

FsↃ and FsↃↃ (not shown): follow similarly.

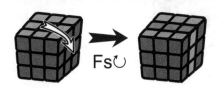

FsↃ

Having problems with the slice moves? You're not alone.

The slice moves get scant respect among the Cube community. The reasons for this are twofold: the speed-solvers don't like slice moves because they can't be executed with one finger quickly, and the theoreticians don't like them because they like keeping the center face cubies stationary so that notation is simpler.

But the slice move is excellent for new solvers trying to understand the Cube, for one simple reason—*the slice moves don't disturb the corner cubies.* Since solving the 3×3×3 is just doing the 8 corners and 12 edges, using moves that only affect edges allow for beginners to more easily follow what's going on in these sequences and understand how they work. This becomes even more invaluable when you move up to the bigger Cubes.

More on this on the next page.

Slices Made Simple.

Slice moves may be easy to visualize, but having an easy-to-visualize move isn't much use if you can't execute the move cleanly and simply.

So, here's a quick guide on how to make some slice moves:

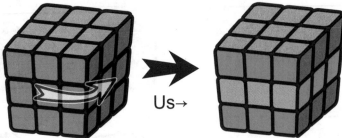

Us→

To do Us→, hold the U layer steady with your left hand, while your right hand grips the Us and D (Down) layers. Your right thumb should be between both layers, while your right index and middle fingers are on the Us and D layers, respectively.

Turn both the Us and D layers to the right a quarter-turn.

Without releasing the Cube, shift your right thumb down a bit, and release pressure on your right index finger.

Now turn the D layer back left, using just your right thumb and middle fingers. (You can slide the ring finger of your left hand down a bit to keep the Us layer from turning.)

This two-turn combination should perform Us→ suitably. Practice this (and the moves on the next page) a few times to make sure you have the movement down pat as one fluid motion.

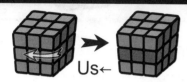

Us←

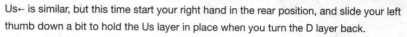

Us← is similar, but this time start your right hand in the rear position, and slide your left thumb down a bit to hold the Us layer in place when you turn the D layer back.

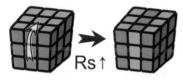

Rs↑

Rs↑ can be done by holding the L layer with your left hand, while the right hand turns both the Rs and R layer up, then the R layer down after retracting the right-hand grip a bit. (The reverse, Rs↓, can be done similarly.)

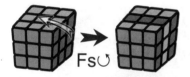

Fs↺

Fs↺ is a bit trickier to deal with. You can either use a similar method to the Us and Rs slice moves, where the left hand holds one face steady while the right hand does a back-and-forth turn, or you can use this alternate method:

Grip the L layer with the left hand, making sure not to touch the Fs slice.

Have your right hand in a "claw" position, where your thumb is on the D (down) side of the DR cubie, and your index and ring fingers are on the U side of the UFR and BFR corner cubies.

With one move, squeeze the "claw" by pulling your right thumb up. This should make Fs↺ in just one move!

(To do Fs↺, simply hold the "claw" upside-down, with your thumb on UR, and pinch the "claw" closed in the same way.)

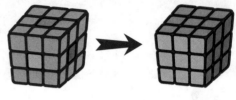

3.1
Solve Corners in One Layer

The 3×3×3 has center face cubies that will determine what the color arrangement in the solved cube should look like. Match every cubie up with the center face cubies, and the Cube is solved.

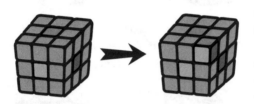

3.1.0

Solving the First Corner

But let's start out with the modest goal of just getting one corner cubie to match the center cubies next to it. Try this on your own first; this is a good exercise to get familiar with the peculiarities of the Cube.

> **No, really, go on and try it!**
> (Also, this seems like a good time to tell you that boxes with an exclamation point, like this one, denote "checkpoints" where it's a good place to stop, review what you've done, and give yourself a pat on the back.)

There are a few different ways to go about this, but we'd like to tell you about one of them that doesn't occur to most people:

Move the center cubies to match the corner, instead of the other way around.

Pick up your cube, and look at the UFR corner cubie, the cubie common to the U (Up), F (Front), and R (Right) face. Look at the color that is on the U side of that cubie (in our example, we're using pink). Find the center cubie that has that color.

If that center cubie is on the R, D, or L face, simply repeat Fs↻ to bring it to the U face.

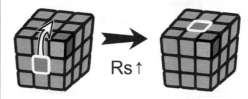

Fs↻

The duplication of D on both lists is not a mistake, if you think about it.

If it is on the F, D, or B face, simply repeat Rs↑.

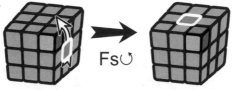

Rs↑

Once the U face cubie is in position, repeat Us→ until the F and R face cubies match the UFR corner cubie.

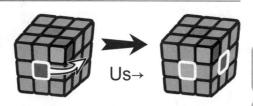

Us→

Great!
You've now positioned (and oriented) the UFR cubie correctly. Now let's move on to another corner cubie, which will require a different approach.

It's remotely possible that no amount of Us→ moves will get the F and R center cubies to match up—because someone has switched the stickers on the cube.

Turn the *entire Cube* (clockwise from the top) so that the UFR cubie is now the UFL cubie.

Our next goal is to find the cubie that should go in the (new) UFR position and solve that. It should be another corner cubie with the U and F color (pink and purple in our example), and the third color should match our new R color (cyan in our example). Once you have found the cubie, see if you can get it there yourself without disturbing the UFL cubie or moving the face cubies. If you're stuck (or even if you're not), go on and read our method in the next section.

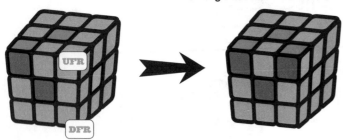

3.1.1

Solving a Second Cubie—the UFR Corner Cubie

Assuming the UFR-colored cubie isn't in the correct place already, your first step should be to put it in the DFR position. You should be able to do this without disturbing the UFL cubie, by simply turning the B (back) face, R (right) face, and D (down) face as needed. Here's how:

If the cubie is anywhere on the Down layer, simply doing D→ (turning the Down layer to the right) repeatedly will bring the cubie to the DFR position eventually.

If the cubie is in the UBR position, then R↓↓ will bring it to the DFR position.

And if the cubie is hiding in the UBL position, then you can turn the B (back) 180° to bring it to the Down layer, then turn the Down layer to bring it to the DFR position.

Now that you have the cubie in the DFR position, here's a simple sequence that swaps the UFR cubie with the DFR cubie. (In the diagram, we've colored those two cubies one consistent color so you can see how they swap.)

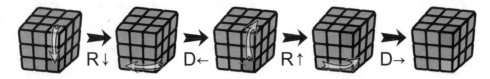

$$A_1 = R{\downarrow}\ D{\leftarrow}\ R{\uparrow}\ D{\rightarrow}$$

This is the first useful move sequence in the book. We'll give the sequence the name A_1.

All right!
You've just learned your first sequence. Practice it a few times if you want; we'll see it again.

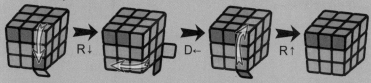
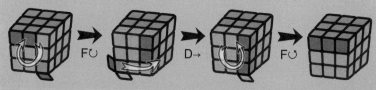
Using the four-move sequence* A_1, you should not have trouble getting the cubie from DFR to UFR (its correct position), but it is possible that the cubie is in the wrong orientation. What can we do about that?

The answer is: by simply repeating A_1, we have a move sequence that twists the UFR cubie counterclockwise. Let's call this sequence A_2 (see the orange box shown on the right).

If the UFR cubie is still in the wrong orientation after A_2, another application of A_2 should fix it:

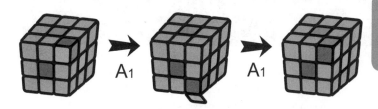

$$A_2 = A_1 A_1 =$$
$$R↓ \ D← \ R↑ \ D→$$
$$R↓ \ D← \ R↑ \ D→$$

If the UFR cubie is still in the wrong orientation after A_2, another application of A_2 should fix it:

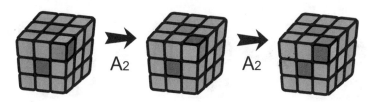

Well done!
The UFR cubie should now be positioned and oriented correctly, and matching the UFL cubie (that you solved in the previous section).

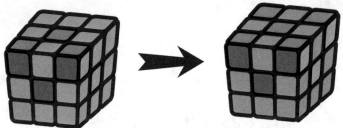

3.1.2

Solving the Rest of the U Layer Corner Cubies

Once you have the UFL and UFR cubies correct, the next thing to do is turn the *entire Cube* clockwise 90° around the U face (as in the diagram below), so that the two cubies you solved (which were the Up and Front cubies) become the Up and Left cubies.

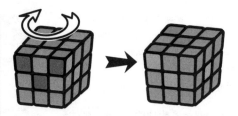

You might have noticed it strange that it takes 8 moves (A_2) to twist the UFR cubie counterclockwise, but 16 moves (A_2A_2) to twist it clockwise. By doing A_2 backward, however, we can do the clockwise twist in 8 moves:

anti-A_2 = D← R↓ D→ R↑ D← R↓ D→ R↑

Also, since we don't really care about the other pieces in the D layer, we can use the F/R mirror trick mentioned in the last box of notes, and combine both sequences to do the twist in just 6 moves:

alternate A_2 = F↻ D← F↻ R↓ D← R↑ (twists UFR counterclockwise)

anti-alternate A_2 = R↓ D→ R↑ F↻ D→ F↻ (twists UFR clockwise)

Reminder:
A_1 = R↓ D← R↑ D→
A_2 = A_1 A_1

This now puts a new color on the F and R faces, which means we have a new UFR position to fill. We can reuse the moves in the previous section to solve the new UFR cubie (put it in the DFR position and repeat A_1/A_2 as necessary to position and orient* it).

By repeating the process again (turning the whole cube and solving the new UFR corner), we can then complete the last corner cubie in the U face.

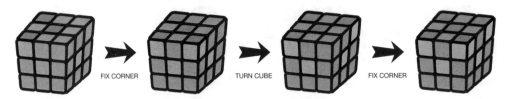

FIX CORNER   TURN CUBE   FIX CORNER

Great!
You've now solved all the corners in one face. Next we'll solve the rest of that face.

3.2
Solve Edges in the Same Layer

There are four "gaps" (positions that need to be filled by the correct cubies) in the U layer, and our next goal is to fill them with the appropriate edge cubies. Look around your cube and see if you can find an edge cubie with the U color (in our picture, pink) that isn't already on the U layer. Turn either the Us slice or the D layer so that the cubie is in one of these two positions:

If the cubie is in the Us slice, bring it to the FR position by turning the Us slice. (Don't worry about the center cubies for now.)

If the cubie is in the D layer, bring it to the FD position by turning the D layer.

Inspect the edge cubie and look at what the other color is on the edge cubie. That should tell you which "gap" in the U layer it should go into. Turn the U layer so that the "gap" is in the UF position. In the example at right, our edge cubie (in the FD position) has a purple sticker, so we position the purple "gap" at the UF position (outlined in white).

Remember, the Us slice is the middle layer sandwiched between the U and the D layers.

Your cube should now look like one of the following four diagrams, based on position and orientation:

① 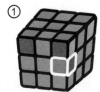 ②  ③  ④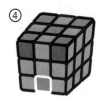

See if you can get the cubie to the "gap" without disturbing the rest of the cube (it's very tricky). Our solutions are on the next page.

$$E_1 = Us \rightarrow F\circlearrowleft Us \leftarrow\leftarrow F\circlearrowleft$$
$$E_2 = Us \rightarrow F\circlearrowleft Us \leftarrow F\circlearrowleft$$
$$E_3 = F\circlearrowleft\circlearrowleft Rs\uparrow F\circlearrowleft\circlearrowleft Rs\downarrow$$
$$E_4 = Rs\uparrow F\circlearrowleft Rs\downarrow F\circlearrowleft$$

Here are the four different sequences we use. Look down the left for your configuration, and use the appropriate sequence to solve the UF edge cubie.

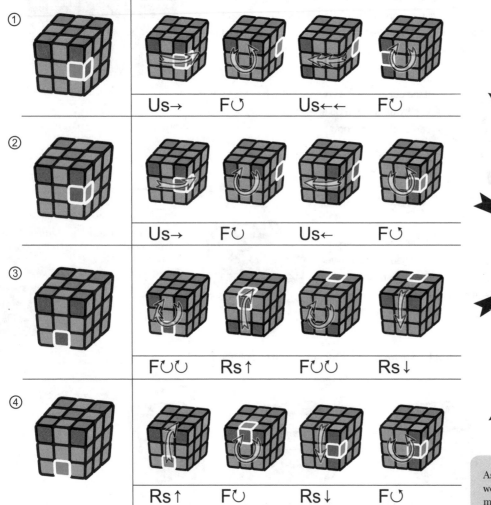

① Us→   F↺   Us←←   F↺

② Us→   F↺   Us←   F↺

③ F↺↺   Rs↑   F↺↺   Rs↓

④ Rs↑   F↺   Rs↓   F↺

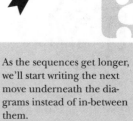

As the sequences get longer, we'll start writing the next move underneath the diagrams instead of in-between them.

To solve the rest of the edge cubies in the U layer, we simply repeat the process:

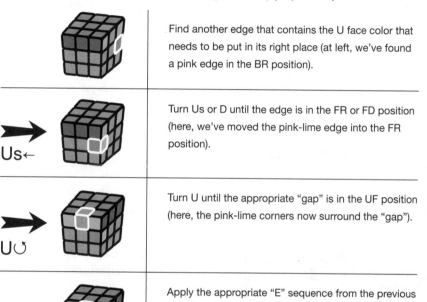	Find another edge that contains the U face color that needs to be put in its right place (at left, we've found a pink edge in the BR position).
Us←	Turn Us or D until the edge is in the FR or FD position (here, we've moved the pink-lime edge into the FR position).
U↺	Turn U until the appropriate "gap" is in the UF position (here, the pink-lime corners now surround the "gap").
E₁	Apply the appropriate "E" sequence from the previous page, and you've solved another edge!

It is possible that you might have U edge cubies that are already in the U layer, but in the wrong position or orientation as seen above. If that happens, simply put that edge cubie in the UF position and use any of the "E" sequences on the last page. It will eject the offending cubie from the U layer, and then you can solve it normally.

Another thing you can try are the "G" sequences found later in this book, in section 3.4.

Now repeat this process for all the edges, and you'll have all four of them solved in no time!*

Congratulations!

You've now solved an entire layer. Give yourself a pat on the back. Now, in preparation for the next step, turn the whole cube upside-down, so that your solved layer (which was U) is now D.

* Advanced solvers will note that the "E" sequences aren't always the fastest sequences that work. For example, F↺ Us→ F↺ is clearly shorter than our E₄. We chose these because the parallelism between these makes them a bit easier to remember. As you get better at visualizing the Cube, try to come up with moves that can move an edge cubie from anywhere to the UF position, without necessarily bringing it to the FR or DR position first.

3.3
Solve the Remaining Corners

The four remaining unsolved corners had better be in the U layer (after all, there's nowhere else for them to go), but they probably are not in their individually correct positions. Even if they are positioned correctly, they probably aren't oriented correctly yet. We will position them correctly first, and then fix their orientation later.

3.3.1

Position the Remaining Corners Correctly

First, let's determine which color needs to end up on top. That's easy; it's the color of the U center (face) cubie (brown in our example). Look at the four U corner cubies and confirm that each one has that color somewhere.* (Ignore the edge cubies on the U layer for now; we'll fix them in section 3.4).

It turns out that, barring rotations of the U layer, these eight coloring arrangements are the only possible ways the color panels of the U face corner cubies can be positioned. One consequence of this is that, if you see a configuration that is not one of these eight (such as having three corner faces on top with the U color), then some joker has probably reassembled your cube in an unsolvable position! (This really happened to one of our testers!)

Now, look at the *other* colors on the four corner cubies. Find a pair of corner cubies on the *same* side (that is, not diagonally apart from each other) that have another color in common—say it's purple, as in the example below. Turn the cube so that the purple center is the F (front) face, and turn the U and D layers so that all the purple corners are on the front face.

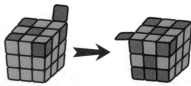

Now you have to find out whether the UFL and UFR cubies are in the correct position (regardless of orientation), or if they have to be swapped. Look at the three colors on the UFR cubie. If you've done everything right up to now, one will be the U color (brown in our example) and one will be the F color (purple in our example). What about the third? Is it the R color (you can determine the R color by looking at the R center cubie or the RD cubies)? If it is, then the UFR is in the correct position (though it may have to be twisted to a new orientation); if the third color on UFR does not match the right bottom row, then we will have to swap UFR and URL using this sequence, which we call C:

matches R;
no swap needed

doesn't match R;
swap needed

$$C = F\circlearrowleft\ U\circlearrowright\ F\circlearrowleft\ U\circlearrowright\ R\uparrow\ U\circlearrowright\ R\downarrow$$

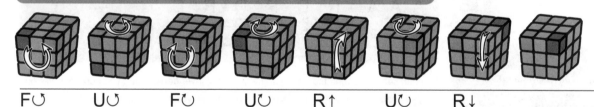

| F⟲ | U⟳ | F⟲ | U⟳ | R↑ | U⟳ | R↓ |

After placing the UFL and UFR cubies correctly, we'll need to look at the other two cubies on the U layer (the UBL and UBR cubies), since they might also need to be swapped. To check this, simply turn the cube 180°, keeping the U face up.

We've colored the two relevant cubies with a uniform color so you can see how they move.

Now the UBL and UBR cubies have become the UFR and UFL cubies. Check to see if they need to be swapped. If so, use sequence C again* to do so.

* Instead of needing to do C twice, you can consider doing:
F⟲ U⟳ R↑ U⟳ R↓ F⟲
which will switch the front corners and the back corners at the same time. Knowing to do this requires you to peek at the back corners before you make the first swap, of course.

Well done!
Now all the corner cubies are placed correctly. Next we'll move on to orienting them correctly.

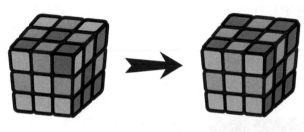

Orient the Remaining Corners Correctly

To twist the corner cubies correctly, we're going to use a simple method that will seem a bit scary at first, because it will appear to mess up the cube. So, first let's start with a little confidence builder.

Remember A_2 from section 3.1.2? Well, it turns out that if you do A_2 three times in a row, the cube returns to the *exact same position* you started with. Try it out now:

After practicing, make sure you understand the rest of the section before trying anything, or you may have to start over!

$$A_2\, A_2\, A_2 = R\!\downarrow D\!\leftarrow R\!\uparrow D\!\rightarrow R\!\downarrow D\!\leftarrow R\!\uparrow D\!\rightarrow$$
$$R\!\downarrow D\!\leftarrow R\!\uparrow D\!\rightarrow R\!\downarrow D\!\leftarrow R\!\uparrow D\!\rightarrow$$
$$R\!\downarrow D\!\leftarrow R\!\uparrow D\!\rightarrow R\!\downarrow D\!\leftarrow R\!\uparrow D\!\rightarrow$$

You can see that during the process, the D (Down) layer goes through a period of unrecognizable chaos, but at the end, everything is back the way it was. Do it some more until you feel comfortable with doing sequence A_2 repeatedly.

Feeling good? Okay, let's continue.

Now, the main useful feature of A_2 is that it twists the UFR corner counterclockwise while leaving the rest of the U layer untouched. (It does stuff to the rest of the cube, but that can get restored by doing A_2 two more times.)

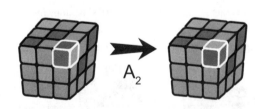

And, doing A_2 *twice* twists the UFR corner counterclockwise twice, which is the same as twisting it clockwise once.

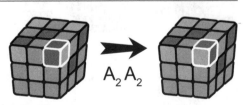

So, if we make some turns to the U layer in between the three times we do A_2, we can control *which* of the corners on the U layer get twisted. Let's look at an example.

In this cube, the brown-cyan-purple corner cubie (at UFR) needs to be twisted once, and the brown-lime-purple corner cubie (at UBR) needs to be twisted twice.

A_2

We start by doing A_2. This twists (once) the brown-cyan-purple corner cubie at UFR, which solves it. (And messes up some cubies in the bottom two layers, which we've marked in black, but we're not worried about them.)

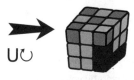

U↺

Then, we do U↺, bringing the brown-lime-purple corner cubie to the UFR position.

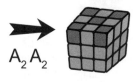

$A_2 A_2$

And now we do $A_2 A_2$. This twists the brown-lime-purple corner cubie at UFR twice, solving it. Now all the corner cubies are oriented correctly and (since we did A_2 three times) the rest of the cube is exactly in the same position it started in!

Keeping that in mind, here's our simple method* to solve all the remaining corners:

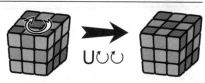

U↺↺

1. Turn U↺ until there is a corner cubie at the UFR position that needs to be twisted.
2. Repeat A_2 until that cubie is fixed.
3. If there are still corner cubies left to fix, go to step 1.

Oh, and one last step—after all the corner cubies are oriented correctly, you'll probably want to turn the U layer to match all the corner colors up with the centers.

This method of reorienting the top corners is simple but can take up to six applications of A_2 and four turns of the U layer, a total of 52 face turns. However, it turns out that $A_2 A_2$ and anti-A_2 have exactly the same effect, so by using anti-A_2 as necessary we can reduce the maximum number of turns to 28. By using the alternate A moves mentioned in a previous note, the number of moves can be reduced even further! Speed-cubers go one step further and memorize moves that twist (and flip) multple cubies at once. If you'd like to experiment in this direction, try playing with this popular sequence that only uses R and U moves (called Sune by speed-solver Lars Petrus when he rediscovered it in 1980):

R↑ U↺ R↓ U↺ R↑ U↺↺ R↓ U↺↺

This sequence twists three cubies in the top layer clockwise while leaving the D layer untouched. All of the eight orientations can be solved by at most two applications of Sune or anti-Sune; can you figure out how?

Outstanding!
All eight corner pieces are now completely solved; that's more than half of the entire cube! Keep up the good work!

3.4
Solve the Opposite Layer Edges

Before you begin this next section, turn the entire cube so that the solved (Down) layer is now the L (Left) layer.

At this juncture, there are only eight unsolved edge cubies left; four on the R layer, and four on the Rs slice. Our next task is to find which four edge cubies that should be on the R layer, and then move them to their proper place *including* correct orientation. (We'll deal with the Rs slice in the next section, so don't worry about messing it up now.)

Identifying which cubies need to go to the R layer should be easy: if the edge cubie has the R color (brown in our pictures), it belongs on the R layer. We'll start by solving one of them.

It is possible, if you're unlucky, that all the R layer edge cubies are already on the R layer, so you won't be able to find one on the Rs slice. If that is the case, fake it by imagining that you've found one, and continue following with us. (The same move that gets an edge cubie *in* to the R layer will also get an edge cubie *out* of the R layer.)

See if you can find such a cubie among the four cubies on the Rs slice. In the diagram at left, we've found a brown-lime edge cubie at the FD position. Take special note of the sticker on this edge cubie that *isn't* the R color (in this case, brown is the R color, so we care about the lime sticker).

Turn the Rs slice until this sticker is on the U face. (Not just the U *layer*, but the U *face*.) It will be in one of the two following positions:

⬅ ①: Up and Front

②: Up and Back ➡

Next, turn the R face until the two corners on top match that sticker color—in other words, the destination "gap" for our edge cubie is now the UR edge. (In the diagrams at right, our sticker is lime, so we've turned the lime corners to the top.)

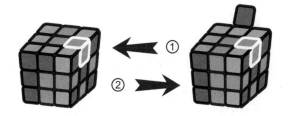

Now, based on whether your position is ① or ②, you are ready to use the appropriate G sequence, both of which move UF, UR, and UB in a cycle, just in different directions:

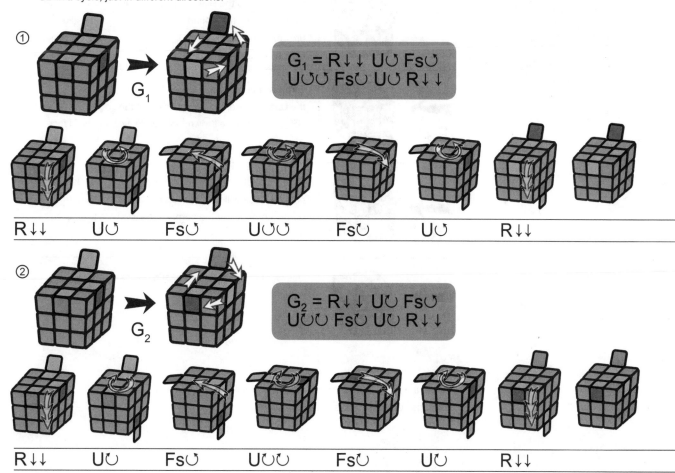

By using G$_1$ or G$_2$, you have now solved one of the four edges on the R layer. Well done! (Or, if we told you to "fake it" earlier, you have now ejected an R layer cube out into the Rs slice, so now you can do the process again, for real this time.)

The next thing to do is to repeat the process:

	Look for another edge cubie on the Rs layer that is supposed to go to the R layer (it will have the R color somewhere). Here we've found the brown-purple edge (R is brown) at the UB position. Look at the non-R color sticker (which is purple here).
Rs↓	Turn Rs until the non-R color sticker (purple here) is on the U face. Here, we've had to move the edge cubie from UB to UF because brown, not purple, was on the U face.
R↓	Turn R until the "gap" for our edge cubie (the stickers on the U face will match) is on the U layer. Here both the purple corners and the purple edge is on the U face.
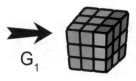 G$_1$	Use G$_1$ or G$_2$ as appropriate, and one more edge cubie is solved.

Repeat the process for all four edges, and you'll have all four edges of the R layer solved in no time*!

Again, just like as in Section 3.2, you might find yourself with some edges already in the R face, but placed incorrectly. As before, you'll have to use a known sequence (in this case, G_1 or G_2) to get it out of its spot, then put it in its spot correctly.

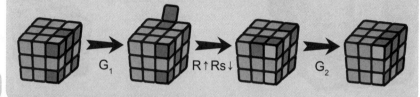

After doing a lot of G sequences, you may notice that it sure seems like you're turning the R face back and forth a lot. And you would be correct. The only reason the $R\downarrow\downarrow$ moves are at the beginning of G is so that all the affected edges are on the U layer, making it easier to visualize. Without those moves, it is the RD edge cubie instead of the RU cubie that gets involved. If you can deal with that and not get confused, you'll save yourself a lot of unnecessary R moves by using the simplified G sequences, as shown to the right.

In fact, if you look carefully, you'll see a similarity between these simplified G sequences and the H sequence in the next section; they're the same sequence, just with an extra U turn and using Fs instead of Rs.

Speed-cubers use this sequence instead:

$$\text{alt-}G_1 = F\circlearrowright\circlearrowright\ U\circlearrowright\ F\circlearrowright\ U\circlearrowright\ F\circlearrowright\ U\circlearrowright$$
$$F\circlearrowright\ U\circlearrowright\ F\circlearrowright\ U\circlearrowright\ F\circlearrowright$$

More moves, but only two faces are turned, making it very easy to do fast. It's very hard to see exactly *how* this sequence accomplishes the same thing as our G_1, though!

$$G_{1s} = U\circlearrowright\ Fs\circlearrowright\ U\circlearrowright\circlearrowright\ Fs\circlearrowright\ U\circlearrowright$$
$$G_{2s} = U\circlearrowright\ Fs\circlearrowright\ U\circlearrowright\circlearrowright\ Fs\circlearrowright\ U\circlearrowright$$

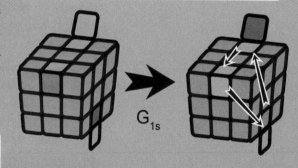

Way to Go!
With four more edges solved, you've now completed two outside layers. Only four pieces remain.

3.5
Position the Remaining Edges

First, turn the Rs slice so that the centers match up:

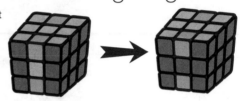

Now, by inspecting the remaining four edge cubies, you should be able to tell which ones are in the correct position, and which ones are not. It's possible for an edge cubie to be in the correct position but "flipped" (oriented the wrong way); count those as correct; we'll deal with the "flipping" in section 3.6. Count how many edge cubies are in the correct position, and look up the appropriate section below.

Four Edges in the Correct Position
If all four of your edge cubies are already in the correct position, great! Move on to section 3.6.

One Edge in the Correct Position
If only one of your edge cubies is correct, then the other three need to be cycled (this is called a "permutation"). Reorient your cube so that the correct edge cubie is in the BD (back-and-down) position. If the permutation you need is "upward" (FD needs to go to FU which needs to go to BU), you can use sequence H:

$$H = U\circlearrowleft\circlearrowleft \; Rs\uparrow \; U\circlearrowleft\circlearrowleft \; Rs\downarrow$$

| U↺↺ | Rs↑ | U↺↺ | Rs↓ |

If you need a "downward" permutation, you have several choices:

1. You can reorient your cube so that the U and F faces are switched, then do H just once.

2. You can do H twice.

3. You can do the inverse of H (Rs↑ U↺↺ Rs↓ U↺↺).

Choose whichever is easiest for you.

Zero Edges in the Correct Position

If none of your edges are correct, you'll have to do a bit more work.* Repeat sequence H (in the previous section) until one edge is correct, then (as per the previous section) put that edge in the BD position and apply H as necessary.

If exactly two of your edges are correct, some practical joker has probably disassembled your cube and put it back together in an impossible-to-solve configuration, as there is no way to swap just two edges with just normal turns.

If exactly three of your edges are correct, some practical joker has probably swapped the stickers of your cube with the stickers of another cube. (Think about it – how can just one item be wrong if there's no other place for it to go?)

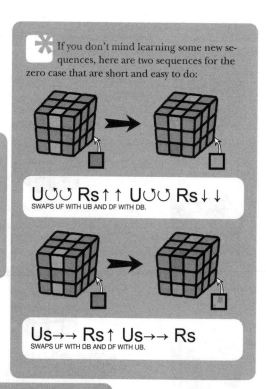

* If you don't mind learning some new sequences, here are two sequences for the zero case that are short and easy to do:

U↺↺ Rs↑↑ U↺↺ Rs↓↓
SWAPS UF WITH UB AND DF WITH DB.

Us→→ Rs↑ Us→→ Rs
SWAPS UF WITH DB AND DF WITH UB.

Almost There!
There's a one-in-eight chance that your cube is already solved. But in case it isn't, flip the page to the last section.

If an odd number of edge cubies are flipped, your cube has been tampered with and cannot be solved using only face turns.

3.6
Orient the Remaining Edges

If your cube isn't solved yet, then either two or four of the edge cubies are flipped—an even number.

Our approach here is going to be very similar to how we handled the corner cubie twisting in section 3.3.2—a move sequence that will flip one edge in a layer while leaving the rest of the cube in what seems like chaos. Then, another move sequence that flips the edge back and restores the rest of the cube.

Let's run through an example first.

Suppose that you need to flip the FD (purple-lime) edge cubie and the UB (cyan-tan) edge cubie.

First, do Rs↑ so that the purple-lime edge (an edge that needs to be flipped) is in the UF position, so we can prepare to flip it.

Then, do sequence K₁ (no, we haven't told you what K₁ is yet), which inverts the UF edge and messes up the rest of the cube (but note how nice the Rs slice looks!).

Then, do Rs↓↓ to bring the other edge cubie, cyan-tan, to the UF position.

Then, do sequence K₂, which not only inverts the cyan-tan UF edge, but also cleans up the rest of the cube.

One final adjustment to the Rs layer (Rs↑), and we're done!

Ready for the real thing now? To review:

1. Turn Rs↑ until there is a edge cubie at the UF position that needs to be flipped.
2. Make the move sequence K₁.
3. Turn Rs↑ until there is another edge cubie at the UF position that needs to be flipped…
4. Make the move sequence K₂.
5. If there are still edge cubies left to fix*, go to step 1.
6. Turn Rs (cancelling out moves you made in steps 1 and 3) until the cube is solved.

Okay, we think you're ready for the real sequences now.

$K_1 = U\circlearrowleft\ F\circlearrowleft\ R\downarrow\ U\circlearrowleft\ F\circlearrowleft$

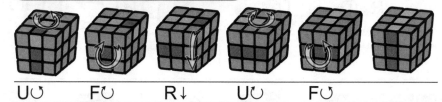

| U↺ | F↺ | R↓ | U↺ | F↺ |

$K_2 = \text{anti-}K_1 = F\circlearrowleft\ U\circlearrowleft\ R\uparrow\ F\circlearrowleft\ U\circlearrowleft$

| F↺ | U↺ | R↑ | F↺ | U↺ |

Flipping two opposite edges on the same face using "K" sequences takes 14 face-turns, which is actually the fewest number of turns possible. But to flip all four edges on the center slice, "K" sequences end up requiring 28 turns (24 if you're crafty). The theoretical minimum is only 18. Here's one such sequence; see if you can figure out how it does what it does.

U↺ R↓ U↺ Rs↓ F↺ Rs↓ F↺
Rs↓ F↺ Rs↓ F↺ U↺ R↑ U↺

All Done!

Congratulations, you've now done something that few can boast to do (yet)—solve the Cube!

All the Sequences for Solving the 3×3×3

Here's a review of all the sequences we've covered. Most of these sequences will mess up sections of the cube; we've colored those sections in black. (Traditional "Singmaster" notation versions of the sequences are given in small print beneath the sequence.)

$$A_1 = R\downarrow\ D\leftarrow R\uparrow\ D\rightarrow$$

R'D'RD

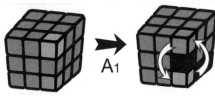

A1

ALSO MESSES UP THE DLB AND DB CUBIES

$$A_2 = R\downarrow\ D\leftarrow R\uparrow\ D\rightarrow$$
$$R\downarrow\ D\leftarrow R\uparrow\ D\rightarrow$$

R'D'RDR'D'RD→

REPEATING A₂ THREE TIMES WILL RESTORE WHAT IT MESSES UP.

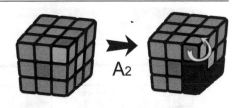

A2

$$E_1 = Us\rightarrow F\cup\ Us\leftarrow\leftarrow F\cup$$
$$E_2 = Us\rightarrow F\cup\ Us\leftarrow F\cup$$
$$E_3 = F\cup\cup\ Rs\uparrow\ F\cup\cup\ Rs\downarrow$$
$$E_4 = Rs\uparrow\ F\cup\ Rs\downarrow\ F\cup$$

UD'L'U2D2R
UD'LU'DF'
F2LR'D2L'R
LR'DL'RF'

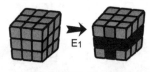

E1

ALSO MESSES UP LB, L, AND B

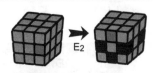

E2

ALSO MESSES UP THE LB EDGE CUBIE

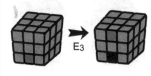

E3

ALSO MESSES UP THE DB EDGE CUBIE

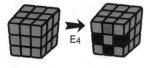

E4

ALSO MESSES UP THE DB EDGE CUBIE

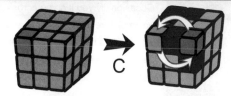

$C = F\circlearrowleft U\circlearrowleft U\circlearrowleft F\circlearrowleft U\circlearrowleft$
$R\uparrow U\circlearrowleft R\downarrow$

F'U'FURUR'

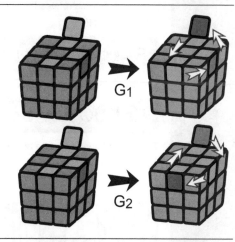

$G_1 = R\downarrow\downarrow U\circlearrowleft Fs\circlearrowleft$
$U\circlearrowleft\circlearrowleft Fs\circlearrowleft U\circlearrowleft R\downarrow\downarrow$
$G_2 = R\downarrow\downarrow U\circlearrowleft Fs\circlearrowleft$
$U\circlearrowleft\circlearrowleft Fs\circlearrowleft U\circlearrowleft R\downarrow\downarrow$

R2U'FB'R2F'BU'R2
R2UFB'R2F'BUR2

THE G SEQUENCES ARE INVERSES OF EACH OTHER

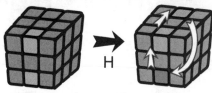

$H = U\circlearrowleft\circlearrowleft Rs\uparrow U\circlearrowleft\circlearrowleft Rs\downarrow$

U2LR'F2L'R

$K_1 = U\circlearrowleft F\circlearrowleft R\downarrow U\circlearrowleft F\circlearrowleft$
$K_2^1 = F\circlearrowleft U\circlearrowleft\circlearrowleft R\uparrow F\circlearrowleft U\circlearrowleft$

U'FR'UF'
FU'RF'U

THE K SEQUENCES ARE INVERSES OF EACH OTHER

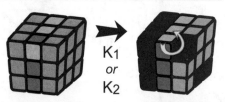

Bonus Section: Orienting the Center Face Cubies

Occasionally you'll come across a Cube where one or more of the center face cubies has a picture or words on it, and therefore must be oriented correctly in the solution. We won't give a thorough treatment of how to reorient all the center faces, but here are two sequences (and their theories) that, when applied correctly, can solve all arrangements of center orientations in at most six applications.

The first sequence rotates the U center face 180° by using the R and L layers to spin the cubies around it:

$$R\downarrow L\uparrow \ U\circlearrowleft\circlearrowright \ R\uparrow L\downarrow \ U\circlearrowright \ R\downarrow L\uparrow \ U\circlearrowleft\circlearrowright \ R\uparrow L\downarrow \ U\circlearrowright$$

The second sequence turns the F center clockwise and the R center counterclockwise:

$$Rs\uparrow \ U\circlearrowright \ Rs\downarrow \ Us\leftarrow \ Rs\uparrow \ U\circlearrowright \ Rs\downarrow \ Us\rightarrow$$

This second one has some principles that are worth diagramming—it's based on the same concept of using sequence A_2 to twist corner cubies and sequences K_1 and K_2 to flip edge cubies.

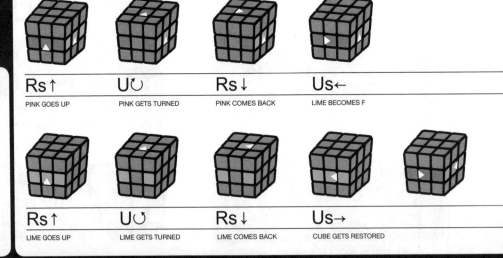

$Rs\uparrow$	$U\circlearrowright$	$Rs\downarrow$	$Us\leftarrow$
PINK GOES UP	PINK GETS TURNED	PINK COMES BACK	LIME BECOMES F

$Rs\uparrow$	$U\circlearrowright$	$Rs\downarrow$	$Us\rightarrow$	
LIME GOES UP	LIME GETS TURNED	LIME COMES BACK	CUBE GETS RESTORED	

Note that you can easily adapt this sequence to handle any two center faces on the Us layer, just by adjusting how much you move Us in steps 4 and 8. You can also change it to turn two center faces 180° instead of 90° just by using $U\circlearrowleft\circlearrowright$ for steps 2 and 6.

Solving the 2×2×2 Cube

How to Solve the 2×2×2 Cube

Solving the 2×2×2 cube is extremely similar to solving the corners of the 3×3×3 cube; you might even say it is identical. There is one difference, though; there are no longer any center face cubies to identify the color of each face! Accordingly, although we will mostly use the techniques mentioned in sections 3.1 and 3.3, we'll make special notes on how to identify the face colors.

2.1
Solving Two Corners

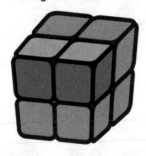

2.2
Solving Four Corners

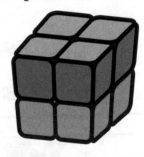

2.3
Position the Remaining Corners

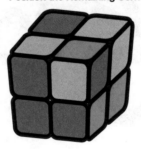

2.4
Orient the Remaining Corners

2.1
Solving Two Corners

This should be easy (especially if you can solve the 3×3×3 cube), but if you're having trouble getting started, try this:

Hold the cube in any position, and look at the UFL (Up/Front/Left) cubie. Let's just say that this corner is correct, and everything else has to match it.

Specifically, we now have a U color (cyan in the example), and an F color (purple in the example).

Hunt around for another cubie that also has the U color and the F color. (Don't lose your UFL cubie, though!) This other cubie will need to go to the UFR position.

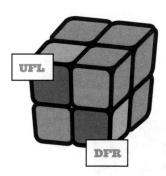

If it's not already there, you can make partial progress by getting it the DFR position. You should be able to do this without disturbing the UFL cube, by simply turning the B (back) face and D (down) face as needed. (If it's on the D layer, just turn the D layer; otherwise, turn the B layer 180° and it will go on the D layer, then turn the D layer as needed.)

Two corners are now solved. Easy!

Now go to section 3.1.1 (on page 82), and follow those instructions to solve the cubie. If you've read that already and just want a refresher, the basic gist is to repeat sequence A₁ until you're done:

$$A_1 = R\downarrow \ D\leftarrow \ R\uparrow \ D\rightarrow$$

2.2
Solving Four Corners

This is pretty much identical to section 3.1.2 (on page 84). Turn the U layer so that a new UFR location needs to be solved, get the appropriate cubie into the DFR position, and repeat sequence A$_1$. Do the same for the fourth corner.

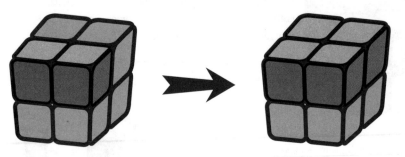

===

2.3
Position the Remaining Corners

Before starting this step, turn over your Cube, so that the layer you've solved is now the D (Down) layer. This part is pretty much the same as section 3.3.1 (on page 88), except that's it's not as obvious what color the U face is suppoed to be.

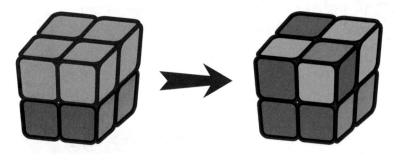

The secret is that the U face color is the only color that is common to all four unsolved corners. The arrangement should be similar to one of those depicted here on the right (and to the equivalent pictures in section 3.3.1).

Knowing what the U color is, you should have no problem following the rest of the instructions in section 3.3.1—find two adjacent cubies with a shared (non-U) color; match them with the D layer, then use sequence C to swap them if necessary. Repeat with the other two cubies.

The equivalent pictures for the 3×3×3 can be seen inside a side-box on page 88.

C = F↺ U↻ F↺ U↻ R↑ U↻ R↓

On the 3×3×3, C was one of the most "destructive" sequences; as in, it disturbed the most other cubies for its length. Here, though, it only interferes with the UBL cubie and mixes up some orientation. If you want a sequence that doesn't affect orientation, it'll be twice as long:

F↺ U↻ F↺ U↻ F↺ R↓ F↺ U↻ F↺ U↻ F↺↻ R↑

All cubies are now positioned correctly. Now onto orientation!

2.4
Orient the Remaining Corners

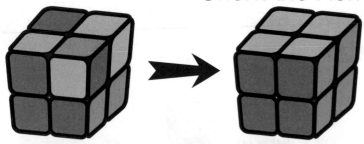

This part is pretty much same as 3.3.2 (on page 90); twist the UFR corner to its correct orientation by repeating sequence A_2, then turn the U layer to put a new cubie in the UFR corner, repeat.

$$A_2 = R\downarrow\ D\leftarrow\ R\uparrow\ D\rightarrow\ R\downarrow\ D\leftarrow\ R\uparrow\ D\rightarrow$$

And the cube is solved!

Here's a review of all the sequences used in the solution for the 2×2×2 cube. Most of these sequences will mess up sections of the cube; we've colored those sections in black.

$$A_1 = R\downarrow\ D\leftarrow\ R\uparrow\ D\rightarrow$$

ALSO MESSES UP THE DLB CUBIE (NOT SHOWN)

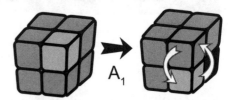

$$A_2 = R\downarrow\ D\leftarrow\ R\uparrow\ D\rightarrow$$
$$R\downarrow\ D\leftarrow\ R\uparrow\ D\rightarrow$$

REPEATING A_2 THREE TIMES WILL RESTORE WHAT IT MESSED UP

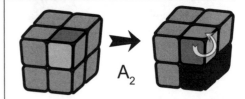

$$C = F\circlearrowleft\ U\circlearrowleft\ F\circlearrowleft\ U\circlearrowleft$$
$$R\uparrow\ U\circlearrowleft\ R\downarrow$$

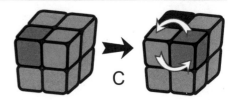

Solving the 4×4×4 Cube

Our method
of approach
will be as
follows:

4.1
Solve the U Face Cubies

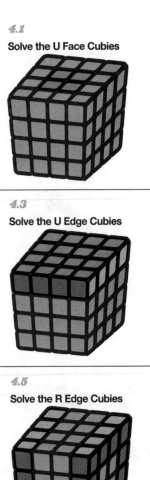

4.2
Solve the U Corner Cubies

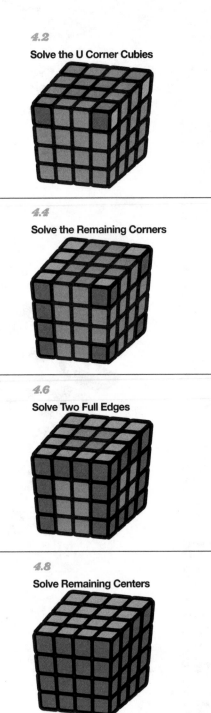

4.3
Solve the U Edge Cubies

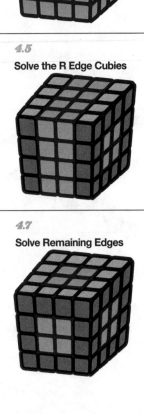

4.4
Solve the Remaining Corners

4.5
Solve the R Edge Cubies

4.6
Solve Two Full Edges

4.7
Solve Remaining Edges

4.8
Solve Remaining Centers

4.0
More on Slice Moves

The solution for the 4×4×4 cube assumes that you're already read our solution to 3×3×3 and understand our notation. The only new notation we need to deal with is that now there are twice as many slices. We'll show diagrams for how to deal with slices parallel to the U face; the equivalents for the other directions should be no problem for you.

U2→: Move the second layer (slice) from the top toward the right.

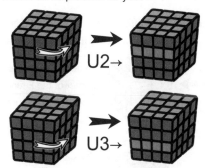

U3→: Move the third layer (slice) from the top toward the right.

U2 and D3 are equivalent, and same goes for lots of other pairs (e.g., L2 and R3). Which one we use in describing moves will be based on which one seems easier for you to remember.

Uu→: Move the first *and* the second layer from the top toward the right. (U+U2)

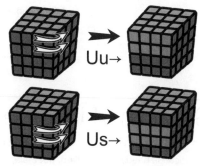

Us→: Move the second and the third layer from the top toward the right. (U2+U3)

The reason we now reuse Us to refer to *two* slices is that in the 4×4×4, as long as you always keep the middle two slices together, the cube becomes equivalent to a 3×3×3, albeit with a visually obese middle layer. This means all of the old sequences we learned earlier will still work fine, as long as we know we're moving two edges together. (And although we won't use it, moving the top *three* layers together to the right would be Uuu→ in our notation.) And now, on to the solution!

4.1
Solve the U Face Cubies

Since the 4×4×4 cube doesn't have a center face cubie, let's start "making" one by matching four identically-colored face cubies together. This should be pretty easy. One way to do it is as follows:

Step 1. Get a pair of adjacent face cubies in the U face.

Step 2. Get a matching pair of adjacent face cubies on the F face (without disturbing the U face cubies you already have).

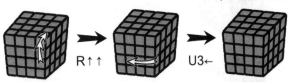

To get a face cubie from the R, L, or B face into the lower-left corner of the F face, turn the face it is on until the cubie is in the lower-left, then turn U3 until it is on the F face.

You can use a similar move with U2 instead of U3 if you need the upper-left corner of the F face, or R2 if you need to get the cubie from the U or D face.

Step 3. Turn the U and F faces so that the U cubies are on R3 and the F cubies are on R2. Then do Rr↑ to bring them all together.

4.2
Solve the U Corner Cubies

This is pretty much identical to section 3.1.2 on page 84. Turn the U layer so that a new UFR location needs to be solved, get the appropriate cubie into the DFR position, and repeat sequence A_1. Do the same for the fourth corner.

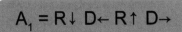

$$A_1 = R{\downarrow}\ D{\leftarrow}\ R{\uparrow}\ D{\rightarrow}$$

4.3
Solve the U Edge Cubies

For the most part, we're going to use a similar technique to that of section 3.2 on page 85, but before we go into that there is a small caveat special to the larger cubes that is worth emphasizing:

 It is physically impossible to "flip" a side edge cubie!

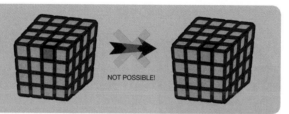

NOT POSSIBLE!

The reason for this is that although the side edge cubies may *look* symmetric, they are internally *not* symmetric. One side of them is closer to the center and it will always stay closer to the center no matter how you manipulate the cube. It might help to imagine a mark at the center of each edge:

If flipping a side edge cubie were possible, then its mark would have to somehow get to the side toward the corner—but you can see for yourself how no move will ever change where the marks are. In other words, side edge cubies have a **chirality**.

If you see an edge cubie on the 4×4×4 that looks "flipped," it is merely in the wrong location and needs to be in the other spot on the same edge.

There are many sequences that will do this. One of the simplest ones is U↻ R↓F↻.

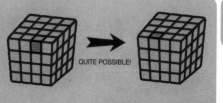

QUITE POSSIBLE!

In any case, our solving technique is the same as in section 3.2 (found on page 85):

1. Turn the U2, U3, or D layer until the edge piece you want is on the FR or FD edge.

2. Turn the U layer until the "hole" you want is on the UF edge.

3. Use a short sequence to bring the edge into the "hole."

Here are the sequences you'll need:

When the destination is the left edge cubie of the UF edge:

① FR, lower: U3→ F↺ U3←← F↺

② FR, upper: U2→ F↺ U2← F↺

③ FD, right: F↺ R↑↑ U3→→ R↑↑ F↺

④ FD, left: R3↑ F↺ R3↓ F↺

When the destination is the right edge cubie of the UF edge:

⑤ FR, upper: U2→ F↺ U2←← F↺

⑥ FR, lower: U3→ F↺ U3← F↺

⑦ FD, left: F↺ R↑↑ U2→→ R↑↑ F↺

⑧ FD, right: R2↑ F↺ R2↓ F↺

Careful readers will notice the similarities between these moves and the "E" sequences, although ③ ⑦ have been changed since the version in section 3.2 disturbs the other UF edge cubie.

After repeating this (at most) 8 times, you should have the entire U layer solved!

Note that there isn't a center face cubie to guide you, so you'll have to use the technique in section 2.3 (on page 106) to guide you.

4.4
Solve the Remaining Corners

This part is the same as section 3.3 on page 88.

Use sequence C to swap corners and A_2 to twist:

$$C = F\circlearrowleft U\circlearrowleft F\circlearrowleft U\circlearrowleft R\uparrow U\circlearrowleft R\downarrow$$
$$A_2 = R\downarrow D\leftarrow R\uparrow D\rightarrow R\downarrow D\leftarrow R\uparrow D\rightarrow$$

 Before starting 4.5, reorient your Cube so that the solved layer is the L layer.

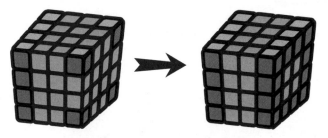

4.5
Solve the R Edge Cubies

We're going to solve these edge cubies by revisiting our old friends from section 3.4 (found on page 92):

$$G_1 = R\downarrow\downarrow U\circlearrowleft Fs\circlearrowleft$$
$$U\circlearrowleft\circlearrowleft Fs\circlearrowleft U\circlearrowleft R\downarrow\downarrow$$

$$G_2 = R\downarrow\downarrow U\circlearrowleft Fs\circlearrowleft$$
$$U\circlearrowleft\circlearrowleft Fs\circlearrowleft U\circlearrowleft R\downarrow\downarrow$$

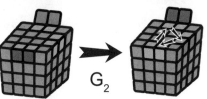

G_1

G_2

 Don't forget that Fs* means *both* middle slices (F2+F3)!

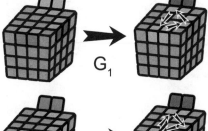 Tired of Fs moves? Read the starred box at the end of section 3.4.

These sequences allow us to move a pair of edge cubies that are on the R2 and R3 slices into the appropriate position onto the R face layer. The only tricky part is getting the cubies to line up.

Pick any edge on the R layer and look for the two edge cubies that need to go into that edge. If the two edge cubies are on the R2 and R3 layer, great! You should be able to turn R2 and R3 to get them in position for a G move, for example:

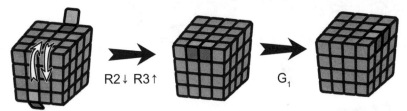

If the two edge cubies are on the same layer (R2 or R3), then turn that layer until both of them are on the U layer (if possible) or just one of them is (if it's not possible to get both of them on the U layer). Then do

$$H_2 = U \cup \cup \; Rs \uparrow \; U \cup \cup$$

and now they should be on separate layers (R2 and R3).
After that, you can pair them up as before.

Finally, if the edge cubies you want are on the R layer, then you'll need to use G_1 or G_2 to get them off of the R layer and onto R2 or R3, for example:

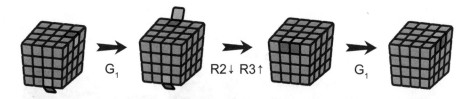

G_1 R2↓ R3↑ G_1

If you would like to explore moving single edge cubies independently, here are two sequences that move three individual edge cubies on the U layer (without disturbing anything else). The first one is shorter, but the second one only moves edge cubies of the same chirality (keeping the U color on top).

Figuring out *why* these two sequences work is outside the scope of this section, but it's worth trying to do on your own so you can make similar sequences!

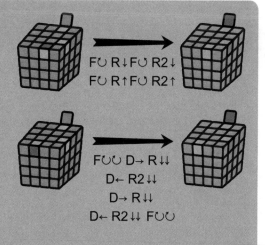

F↺ R↓ F↺ R2↓
F↺ R↑ F↺ R2↑

F↺↺ D→ R↓↓
D← R2↓↓
D→ R↓↓
D← R2↓↓ F↺↺

By judiciously repeating this process (getting two edges to match* on the R2 and R3 layer, then using a G sequence as appropriate), you should be able to solve all the edges on the R layer.

4.6
Solve Two Full Edges

If you've mastered the last section, getting one more edge solved should be pretty simple. Choose any edge and match up the two edge cubies as per the last section. Then, turn Rs until the edge matches with the L and R layers.

Sometimes the edge you've solved will need to be "flipped." Fix this by putting it in the UF position and doing H_3:

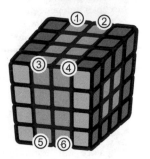

$$H_3 = H_2 \text{ Rs}\uparrow\uparrow = \text{U}\cup\cup \text{ Rs}\uparrow \text{ U}\cup\cup \text{ Rs}\uparrow\uparrow$$

Now that one edge is solved, let's put it out of the way by reorienting the cube so the solved edge is the DB (Down and Back) edge. This leaves the only unsolved edges to be the UB, UF, and DF edges. We'll label them with the numbers ①②③④⑤⑥ as in the diagram to the right, and our next goal will be to get the positions ⑤ and ⑥ (the DF edge) filled correctly.

If ⑤ is in ⑥'s position, or vice versa (you'll be able to tell because it will appear "flipped"), use this sequence* H4 to get it out. (You might even fix the other one!)

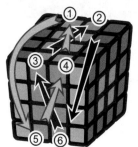

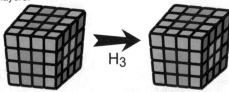

$$H_4 = H_2 \text{ Rs}\downarrow = \text{U}\cup\cup \text{ Rs}\uparrow \text{ U}\cup\cup \text{ Rs}\downarrow$$
$$⑤→④→①→⑤$$
$$⑥→③→②→⑥$$

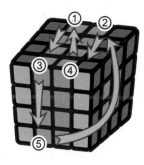

Next, to place ⑤ correctly, use this H_5 (identical to H_4 except that it uses R3 instead of Rs):

$$H_5 = U\,\cup\,\cup\ R3\uparrow\ U\,\cup\,\cup\ R3\downarrow$$
$$⑤\rightarrow②\rightarrow④\rightarrow①\rightarrow③\rightarrow⑤$$

You may need to do this move up to four times, but at least it's easy. (Or you could do anti-H_5 if the cubie is in position ⑤ or ⑥.)

Placing ⑥ uses (you guessed it) a similar sequence we call H_6:

$$H_6 = U\,\cup\,\cup\ R2\uparrow\ U\,\cup\,\cup\ R2\downarrow$$
$$⑥\rightarrow①\rightarrow③\rightarrow②\rightarrow④\rightarrow⑥$$

After this, ⑤ and ⑥ should be correct, and now there are only four more edge cubies to go!

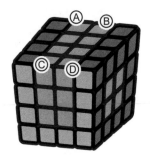

4.7
Solve Remaining Edges

This part is probably the hardest section of the entire solution, as there are 24 ways the four remaining edges can be arranged, and it is not particularly obvious how the solving sequences actually work. Let's start by labelling the four edges Ⓐ Ⓑ Ⓒ Ⓓ. (We could have used ① ② ③ ④ from the last section, but it will be a bit less confusing to start afresh.)

Of the 24 arrangements, 12 of them are "odd" arrangements (they need an odd number of edge swaps to solve, if that makes sense to you), and 12 of them are "even" arrangements. Your first task is to figure out whether your given arrangement is "odd" or "even."

The following 12 arrangements are "odd." You can tell because they either have a single swap or a length-four cycle:

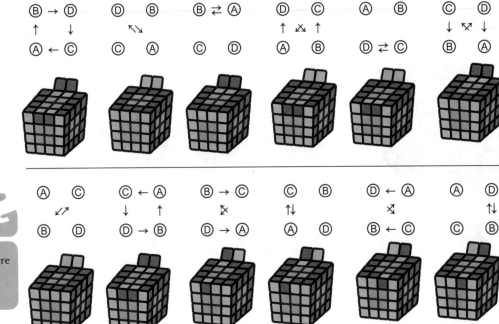

If your arrangement is "odd," you need to make it "even" by using sequence W, shown to the right:

(An alternate version of W, R2↓↓ U↺↺ R2↓ U↺↺ R2↓↓, is easier to memorize but has more slice moves. Use whichever you like.)

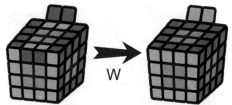

W = Rr↓↓ Uu↺↺
R2↓ Uu↺↺ Rr↓↓

Ⓐ→Ⓑ→Ⓓ→Ⓒ→Ⓐ

(REMEMBER: "UU" AND "RR" MEAN TO
TURN TWO LAYERS TOGETHER AS A GROUP.)

This turns them into one of these "even" arrangements:

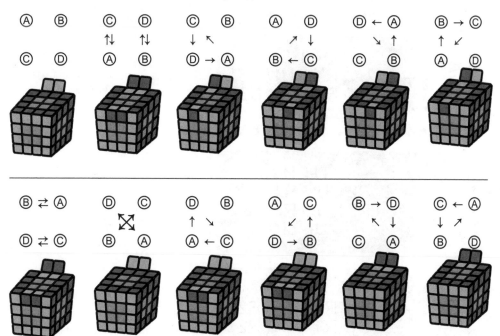

The first arrangement in the upper-left is solved, so we need to only supply answers for the other 11. Of the 11 arrangements, 8 of them (the ones on the right) are all three-cubie cycles, and they can all be solved by variations on the same sequence. We'll show it on the next page.

This is the basic sequence* for a three-cycle.

© B
↓ ↖
D → A

$$T_1 = \begin{array}{l} \text{Rr↓ D→} \\ \text{R3↓ U↺ R↓↓ U↺} \\ \text{R3↑ U↺ R↑↑ U↺} \\ \text{D← Rr↑} \end{array}$$

This comes in three more varieties based on Left-Right symmetry and inversion:

D B
↑ ↘
A ← C

$$T_2 = \begin{array}{l} \text{Rr↓ D→} \\ \text{U↺ R↓↓ U↺ R3↓} \\ \text{U↺ R↑↑ U↺ R3↑} \\ \text{D← Rr↑} \end{array}$$

A D
↗ ↓
B ← C

$$T_3 = \begin{array}{l} \text{Ll↓ D→} \\ \text{R2↓ U↺ R↓↓ U↺} \\ \text{R2↑ U↺ R↑↑ U↺} \\ \text{D← Ll↑} \end{array}$$

A C
↙ ↑
D → B

$$T_4 = \begin{array}{l} \text{Ll↓ D→} \\ \text{U↺ R↓↓ U↺ R2↓} \\ \text{U↺ R↑↑ U↺ R2↑} \\ \text{D← Ll↑} \end{array}$$

*These sequences use the concept of conjugation, which can be thought of as "taking pieces temporarily to locations where the action is and then bringing them back."

Here, the first two moves bring one of the UF edges to the DR position, the next eight moves cycle three edges, and then the last two moves bring the DR edge (now a different cubie) back to the UF position.

The symbol "Ll" is just an "L" followed by a lower-case "L"—in other words, turn both the L and L2 layers together.

D ← A   C ← A
↘ ↑   ↓ ↗
C   B   B   D

B → D   B → C
↖ ↓   ↑ ↙
C   A   A   D

For the other four "three-cycle" arrangements, simply turn the cube 180° around the U face, so that F and B are switched, as well as R and L. Then apply the appropriate T sequence, to the left.

The other three arrangments (the "double swaps") are best solved by learning the three specialized sequences here, all of which are pretty simple (and one you should already know). (Alternatively, you can just use any of the T sequences on the previous page, which will fix one of the four cubies. Then choose the appropriate T sequence again to fix it.)

Ⓑ ⇄ Ⓐ

Ⓓ ⇄ Ⓒ

This is the easiest as it is the equivalent of "two edge flips" as covered in section 3.6. To refresh your memory, the solution from there is:

$$V_1 = K_1 \; Rs{\uparrow} \; K_2 \; Rs{\downarrow}$$
$$= F\circlearrowleft \; U\circlearrowleft \; R{\uparrow} \; F\circlearrowleft \; U\circlearrowleft \; Rs{\uparrow}$$
$$U\circlearrowleft \; F\circlearrowleft \; R{\downarrow} \; U\circlearrowleft \; F\circlearrowleft \; Rs{\downarrow}$$

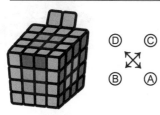

Ⓓ   Ⓒ
   ⤫
Ⓑ   Ⓐ

This sequence* is equivalent to WW (the 180° moves cancel out):

$$V_2 = Rr{\downarrow}{\downarrow} \; Uu\circlearrowleft\circlearrowleft$$
$$R2{\downarrow}{\downarrow} \; Uu\circlearrowleft\circlearrowleft \; Rr{\downarrow}{\downarrow}$$

Ⓒ   Ⓓ
↑↓   ↑↓
Ⓐ   Ⓑ

You can either do V_1V_2, or this shorter sequence:

$$V_3 = F\circlearrowleft\circlearrowleft \; R2{\downarrow} \; F\circlearrowleft\circlearrowleft \; R2{\uparrow}$$
$$R3{\downarrow} \; F\circlearrowleft\circlearrowleft \; R3{\uparrow} \; F\circlearrowleft\circlearrowleft$$

✳ V_2 and V_3 have a small flaw that you probably won't care about unless you're devising your own system—they disturb the arrangement of some face cubies. If you ever decide to use a method where the face cubies are solved first, you might be desirous of equivalents for V_2 and V_3 that don't have this side effect. Here they are:

V_2 (alternate) = Ff$\circlearrowleft\circlearrowleft$ U$\circlearrowleft\circlearrowleft$ Ff$\circlearrowleft$ U$\circlearrowleft\circlearrowleft$ Ff$\circlearrowleft\circlearrowleft$
                 U$\circlearrowleft\circlearrowleft$ Ff$\circlearrowleft\circlearrowleft$ U$\circlearrowleft\circlearrowleft$ Ff$\circlearrowleft$ U$\circlearrowleft\circlearrowleft$ Ff$\circlearrowleft\circlearrowleft$

V_3 (alternate) = F$\circlearrowleft$ U$\circlearrowleft$ R$\uparrow$ U3$\leftarrow\leftarrow$ R$\downarrow$ U$\circlearrowleft$ F$\circlearrowleft$ U$\circlearrowleft\circlearrowleft$
                 F$\circlearrowleft$ U$\circlearrowleft$ R$\uparrow$ U3$\leftarrow\leftarrow$ R$\downarrow$ U$\circlearrowleft$ F$\circlearrowleft$ U$\circlearrowleft\circlearrowleft$

Now all the edges are solved!

4.8
Solve Remaining Centers

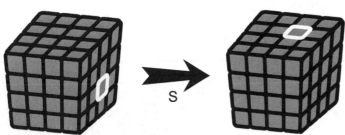

This final section is easier than the others. What we need is a sequence that moves a center cubie from the lower-right (actually DownBack) corner of the Right face to the upper-right (actually RightBack) corner of the Up face:

The basic sequence* we will use to do this moves three center cubies around in a cycle.

$$S = U2\leftarrow R2\downarrow$$
$$U2\rightarrow R\downarrow$$
$$U2\leftarrow R2\uparrow$$
$$U2\rightarrow R\uparrow$$

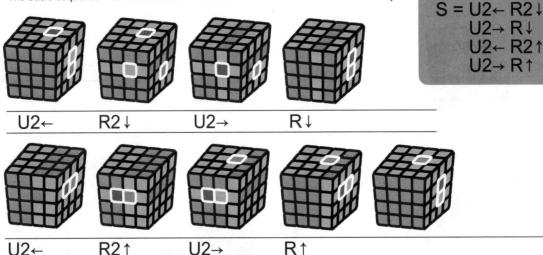

| U2← | R2↓ | U2→ | R↓ |

| U2← | R2↑ | U2→ | R↑ |

Since we were careful to solve the L face cubies way back in 4.1, we can solve all the face cubies by keeping the R face right and moving different faces to the U layer. The general procedure is:

1. Find a misplaced cubie in the R face.
2. Turn the cube so that the destination is in the U face.
3. Turn the R face so that the misplaced cubie is DownBack.
4. Turn the U face so that a destination position is RightBack.
5. Sequence S.
6. Undo the move in step 4.
7. Undo the move in step 3.
8. Repeat from step 1.

Here's an example.

	1. Find a misplaced cubie in the R face.
	2. Turn the Cube so that the destination is in the U face.
	3. Turn the R face so that the misplaced cubie is DownBack.
	4. Turn the U face so that a destination position is RightBack.
	5. Apply Sequence S. If you want, you may want to test out steps 6 and 7 before doing S.
	6. Undo* the move in step 4. Note that this is *before* the reversal of step 3, which is obvious if you think about it.
	7. Undo the move in step 3.

Steps 3-4 and Steps 6-7 are more conjugation!

Occasionally you will reach a situation where all the face cubies in the R face are solved, but some of the other face cubies still need work. (You can avoid this for the most part by not choosing destination positions that have the R color.) If this occurs, you have to to break up your nice R face; move an R face cubie into one of the incorrect face cubies via sequence S. This should move the incorrect face cubie somewhere on the R face, and the solving can continue. Example:

Here the R face is completely solved.

Sequence S pushes an R cube away and a new incorrect cube back onto the R face.

Eventually, you'll place all the face cubies and your Cube is solved!

While a "faces last" approach is the simplest to understand, it also tends to be one of the slower approaches, because the face sequences involves lots of slice moves, each of which requires two effective turns. You can save quite a bit of time if you solve the faces first — but then your edge cubie sequences need to keep the faces untouched, such as the T sequences we've mentioned. More on this in a couple of pages.

Well done! Give yourself a pat on the back.

Bonus Section: Dealing with the "Single Edge Flip"

People who are used to the 3×3×3 Cube often try to solve the 4×4×4 by trying to reduce it to what they know, by matching the face and edge cubies first. They think that then solving it as a 3×3×3 should be simple.

And often, it is. But about half of the time you end up with a situation at the left, where there is an "odd" arrangement (see section 4.7) and no 3×3×3 technique is going to help you.

The reason is that the center face cubies are interchangable, creating an effect where you think they are solved, but actually identical-looking pieces need to be swapped. Our method cleverly gets around this by dealing with the issue before the face cubies are solved.

If you're doing a faces-first solution and just want to fix an oddness problem without redoing a lot of face work, what can you do?

Well, the simplest three-cycle is as follows:

UↃ R↑ UↃ R2↓
UↃ R↓ UↃ R2↑

The first three moves put the lime cubie where the purple cubie is without messing up the rest of the R2 layer. Then the R2 layer is moved so that the pink cubie is where the purple cubie started. Moves 5–7 undo the first three moves, so that the purple cubie comes back, and move 8 restores the R2 layer.

Try to understand how that three-cycle works; it's the fundamental idea behind sequence T, as well as the moves in the starred in section 4.5. By making adjustments (different R turns, different layers), you can adapt it to cycle any three edge cubies you want.

So what about that two-cycle? No series of three-cycles is ever going to solve this, so what to do?

Simple. Turn R2↓, and now your edges have a five-cycle. That can be fixed with three-cycles.

This whole process basically replaces the oddness problem of edges with an oddness problem in faces—now we have four sets of faces in a four-cycle. But this is easily fixed:

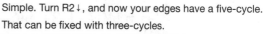

FsↃ R↓↓ FsↃ R2↓ FsↃ R↓↓ FsↃ R2↓
FsↃ R↓↓ FsↃ R2↓ FsↃ R↓↓ FsↃ R2↓

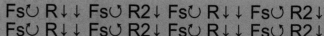

This is actually a five-cycle with pairs of face cubies on the R2 layer and the left pair on the U layer, using the R face as a staging area to swap two such pairs.

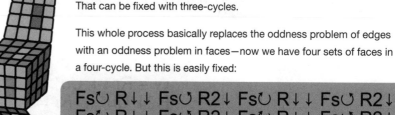

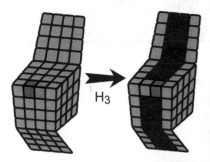

H₃

Here's a review of all the sequences we've covered that are new to the 4×4×4. The rest are covered in the 3×3×3 section. Again, we color in black the cubies that get hurt as a side effect. *(We won't draw the arrows this time; they criss-cross a lot and get really confusing.)*

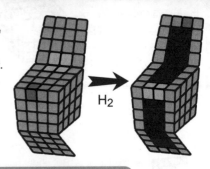

H₂

$$H_2 = U \cup \cup \; Rs\uparrow \; U \cup \cup$$

$$H_3 = H_2 \; Rs\uparrow\uparrow = U \cup \cup \; Rs\uparrow \; U \cup \cup \; Rs\uparrow\uparrow$$

$$H_4 = H_2 \; Rs\downarrow = U \cup \cup \; Rs\uparrow \; U \cup \cup \; Rs\downarrow$$

$$H_5 = U \cup \cup \; R2\uparrow \; U \cup \cup \; R3\downarrow$$

$$H_6 = U \cup \cup \; R3\uparrow \; U \cup \cup \; R2\downarrow$$

$$W = Rr\downarrow\downarrow \; Uu\cup\cup \; R2\downarrow \; Uu\cup\cup \; Rr\downarrow\downarrow$$

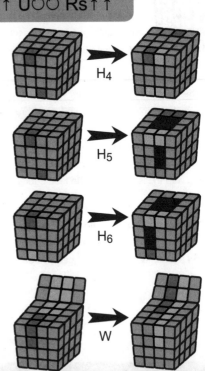

H₄

H₅

H₆

W

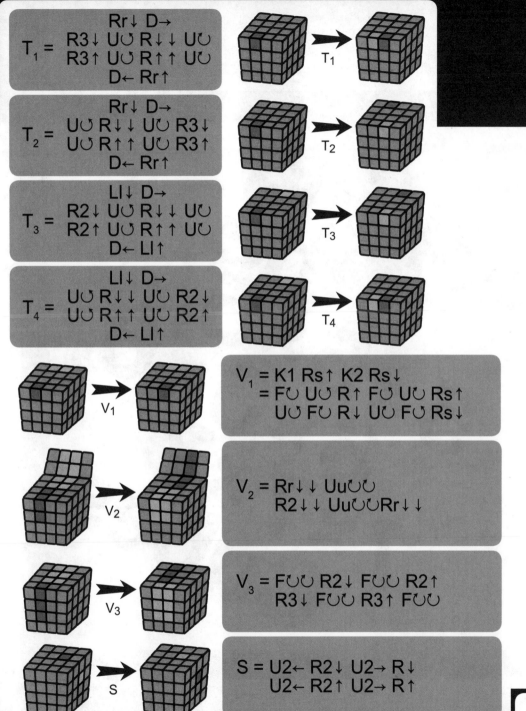

$T_1 =$ Rr↓ D→
R3↓ U↻ R↓↓ U↻
R3↑ U↻ R↑↑ U↻
D← Rr↑

$T_2 =$ Rr↓ D→
U↻ R↓↓ U↻ R3↓
U↻ R↑↑ U↻ R3↑
D← Rr↑

$T_3 =$ Ll↓ D→
R2↓ U↻ R↓↓ U↻
R2↑ U↻ R↑↑ U↻
D← Ll↑

$T_4 =$ Ll↓ D→
U↻ R↓↓ U↻ R2↓
U↻ R↑↑ U↻ R2↑
D← Ll↑

$V_1 =$ K1 Rs↑ K2 Rs↓
= F↻ U↻ R↑ F↻ U↻ Rs↑
U↻ F↻ R↓ U↻ F↻ Rs↓

$V_2 =$ Rr↓↓ Uu↻↻
R2↓↓ Uu↻↻ Rr↓↓

$V_3 =$ F↻↻ R2↓ F↻↻ R2↑
R3↓ F↻↻ R3↑ F↻↻

S = U2← R2↓ U2→ R↓
U2← R2↑ U2→ R↑

129

Solving the 5×5×5, 6×6×6, 7×7×7 Cubes

Assuming you know how to solve the smaller cubes, there are two different methods to generalize our approach the 5×5×5—a "holistic" method and a "reductionistic" method. Choose whichever one appeals to you.

How to Solve the 5×5×5 Cube

The "Holistic" Method (faster but longer to explain)

5.1

Solve the Face Cubies in the U Face

Use methods similar to that of 4.1 to do this. You'll need to construct little "mini-rows" of three face cubies, and then bring them up to the Up face.

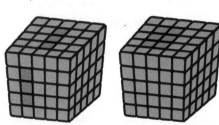

5.2
Solve the U Corners

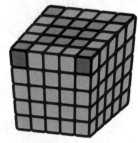

Just like in 4.2 and 3.1.2.

5.3
Solve the U Edges

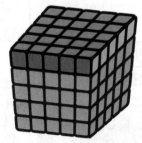

Use 3.2 for the middle edge cubies and 4.3 for the side edge cubies.

5.4
Solve the Remaining Corners

Turn the cube upside-down and solve the remaining corners, just like in section 3.3.

Solve the Opposite Edges

Make the solved face the L face and fill in the edges in the R face, ideally by the same mehod as in 4.5. You might occasionally have a middle edge cubie that needs to be flipped by itself; U↺↺ R3↑ U↺↺ R3↑↑ (a similar sequence appears in 4.6) will flip the UF edge if you need it.

Solve the Remaining Edges

Use 4.6 and 4.7 for the side edges and 3.5 for the center edge cubies.

Solve the Remaining Faces

Sequence S from section 4.8 will basically be all you need, as long as you know how to vary the slice that gets affected. Here are two versions (with R2 vs. R3) to help you:

$$S_2 = U2{\leftarrow}\ R2{\downarrow}\ U2{\rightarrow}\ R{\downarrow}\ U2{\leftarrow}\ R2{\uparrow}\ U2{\rightarrow}\ R{\uparrow}$$

$$S_3 = U2{\leftarrow}\ R3{\downarrow}\ U2{\rightarrow}\ R{\downarrow}\ U2{\leftarrow}\ R3{\uparrow}\ U2{\rightarrow}\ R{\uparrow}$$

And congratulations; you've solved the 5×5×5.

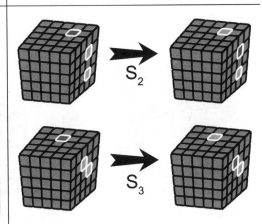

The "Reductionistic" Method (slower but simpler to explain)

5.1

Use the 4×4×4 Solution

Completely ignore the center slices, and solve the cube as if it were a 4×4×4. (As an extra option, during step 4.1, feel free to solve an entire face, including the center slices on that face—this will save you some time when you get to 5.4, below.)

5.2

Solve the Center Face Cubes

Using center slices, match all the centers (you've probably been tempted to match them already by now anyway). If you need help, check out the first part of section 3.1, where center slice moves are used to move the centers around.

5.3

Use the 3×3×3 Solution to Solve the Center Edge Cubies

Treat the cube as a 3×3×3 with "fat" outside layers, and solve the rest of the edges (ignore the unsolved face cubies for now). You should only need sections 3.2, 3.4, 3.5, and 3.6 for this. (The center edge cubies don't have the "oddness" problem that the 4×4×4 has!)

5.4

Solve the Remaining Face Cubies

$$U2_{\leftarrow}\ R3_{\downarrow}\ U2_{\rightarrow}\ R_{\downarrow}$$
$$U2_{\leftarrow}\ R3_{\uparrow}\ U2_{\rightarrow}\ R_{\uparrow}$$

All we need here is a variant on the sequence S used in section 4.8; this one moves three face cubies in a cycle (those highlighted above). By repeating this in the same way as section 4.8, you can solve the rest of the Cube!

How to Solve the 6×6×6 Cube

We'll just present the reductionistic approach here; if you like the holistic approach, you can probably figure it out yourself by now!

6.1

Use the 4×4×4 Solution

Completely ignore the two center slices, and solve the cube as if it were a 4×4×4. (As an extra option, during step 4.1, feel free to solve an entire face, including the center slices on that face—this will save you some time when you get to 6.3, below.)

6.2

Use the 4×4×4 Solution Again

This time, treat the outside layers as "fat" layers, and use the 4×4×4 solution again. Since the "corners" are already solved, you'll only need to deal with the edge sections.

6.3

Use "Sequence S"- like Moves to Solve the Rest

Just as in the 5×5×5, variants on sequence S from section 4.8 can be used to finish the Cube off. The sequence here, for example, cycles the three face cubies highlighted at left.

$$U2{\leftarrow}\ R3{\downarrow}\ U2{\rightarrow}\ R{\downarrow}$$
$$U2{\leftarrow}\ R3{\uparrow}\ U2{\rightarrow}\ R{\uparrow}$$

It's worth mentioning that, although they may look interchangable, the remaining 24 face cubies actually come in two chiralities. (Look "chirality" up if you've never encountered the word before.) The "clockwise" ones (highlighted at right) are always going to stay "clockwise" no matter how you move the layers, so don't try to swap them into the "counterclockwise" positions; it won't work! And with the 6×6×6 solved, we move on...

Astute readers can probably write this section all by themselves...

How to Solve the 7×7×7 Cube

7.1

Use the 6×6×6 Solution

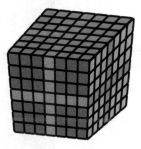

Ignore the middle slices, and … no surprise here. (If you want, you can skip all parts regarding solving the face cubies, and just deal with all of them together at the end.)

7.2

Use the 5×5×5 Solution

We could have said to use the 3×3×3 solution, but this way we make it one less step since we get one set of face cubies for free. Obviously you'll only need steps 5.2–5.4 of the 5×5×5 solution.

7.3

Use "Sequence S"-like Moves to Solve the Rest

Just like section 5.4 again, and the big cube is solved!

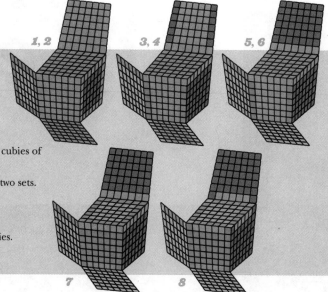

1, 2   3, 4   5, 6

7   8

* The reader might be interested in how Wei-Hwa actually solves the large Cubes. His favorite method is based on two considerations: one, that face-cubie sequences are tedious and so the faces should be solved early; and two, that looking for edge cubies is often the slowest part of the solution. Here's his sequence:

1. Face cubies on one face.

2. Face cubies on opposite face.

3. Three edges on a "solved" face and the two corners between them.

4. Same-colored edges and corners on the opposite face.

5. Two adjacent sets of face cubies of two of those side colors.

6. The edge between those two sets.

7. The last two faces.

8. The last four corners.

9. The remaining edge cubies.

Index, References, and Credits

Photo Credits:

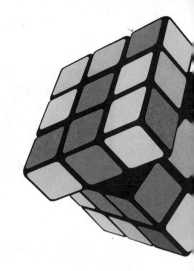

Bandelow, Christoph. *Inside Rubik's Cube and Beyond*. Birkhäuser, Boston, MA, 1982. p. 47

Jack Botermans, p.14–17, 25, 43–46, 50–57, 60–65

Adam Cowan p. 63

Ton Dennenbroek p. 46

Tony Fisher, p. 50

Anthony Greenhill, 62

Geert Hellings, p. 46, 54–55, 60–63

Aleh Hladzilin, p. 60

Lilly Library, p. 24, 33

Uwe Meffert, p. 50

Chris Morgan, p. 20–21, 24, 27–30, 34–39, 42–44, 46–47, 50–51, 53–54, 57–59

Larry Nichols, p. 21

Katsuhiko Okamoto, p. 60

Peter Sebestény, p. 46

Matt Shepit, p. 64

David Singmaster, p. 31–32, 34, 38

Hidetoshi Takeji, p. 61

Frank Tiex, p. 57, 63–65

Seven Towns Ltd., p. 22–23

Lee Tutt, p. 62

Frans de Vreugd, p. 142

Panagiotis Verdes, p. 48

References:

Bandelow, Christoph. *Inside Rubik's Cube and Beyond*. Birkhäuser, Boston, MA, 1982.

Frey, Jr., Alexander and David Singmaster. *Handbook of Cubik Math*. Enslow Publishers, Hillside NJ, 1982.

Rubik, Ernő. Tamás Varga, Gerzson Kéri, György Marx and Tamás Vekerdy. *Rubik's Cubik Compendium*. Oxford University Press, Oxford, 1987.

Singmaster, David. *Notes on Rubik's Magic Cube*. Enslow Publishers, Hillside, NJ, 1981.

About the Authors

Jerry Slocum, a retired Aerospace executive, is a historian, collector, and author specializing in the field of mechanical puzzles. His personal collection of over 31,000 mechanical puzzles is believed to be one of the world's largest. He is the author of twelve earlier books on puzzles including *Puzzles Old and New*, *The 15 Puzzle Book* and *The Tangram Book*. In 2006, Slocum donated his entire puzzle collection and library of over 4,000 puzzle books to the Lilly Library at Indiana University, marking the first time a major collection of puzzles was made available in an academic setting. He also founded The International Puzzle Collectors' Party in 1978 that organizes annual gatherings of as many as 400 puzzle collectors from all over the world.

David Singmaster is a retired professor of mathematics at London South Bank University. From 1978 to 1984, he was the leading spokesperson for Rubik's Cube™. Singmaster wrote the first book on the Cube, *Notes on the 'Magic Cube*,*'* which included his now standard notation for describing the Cube and its solutions. He also wrote the foreword for Erno Rubik's book, *B_v_s Kocka (The Magic Cube)*, and edited the English translation, which was released as in 1987 as *Rubik's Cubic Compendium*. He has one of the world's largest collections of books on recreational mathematics and his on-going annotated bibliography, *Sources in Recreational Mathematics* is a standard resource for puzzlers.

Wei-Hwa Huang is an award-winning American puzzler and member of the US Team for the World Puzzle Federation. He is a four-time World Puzzle Champion, won the US Sudoku Championship in 2008, and was one of the first to have solved a 6x6x6 and 7x7x7 Cube. While an employee at Google, Huang launched the popular *Da Vinci Code Quest*, a set of 24 puzzles, in cooperation with Columbia Pictures.

Dieter Gebhardt is a leading expert in the field of rotational puzzles. Along with Jerry Slocum, he is the co-author of *The Tangram Book*. In 1990, he began writing for *Cubism For Fun*, the leading worldwide magazine for mechanical puzzles which is published by the Nederlandse Kubus Club (Dutch Cube Club). He has now published nearly 70 articles introducing puzzles and presenting their solutions, mostly in the sector of rotational puzzles.

TOP LEFT TO RIGHT:
JERRY SLOCUM,
DAVID SINGMASTER,
WEI-HWA HUANG,
DIETER GEBHARDT,
GEERT HELLINGS

Geert Hellings received his PhD in Physics from the Eindhoven University of Technology in the Netherlands. His interest in rotational puzzles began in the early 1990's after becoming a member of the Nederlandse Kubus Club (Dutch Cube Club) and he is currently the president of the association, which currently has over 500 members around the world. He designed some handcrafted rotational puzzles, the most significant being the uniform 2x2x4, the 2x2x6, and the Rainbow Octahedron.